THE PLEASURES OF COARSE FISHING
An Angler's Pitch

Titles in the Spellmount Country List:

Royalty in Tunbridge Wells
The Shires in our Lives (Heavy Horses)
Memories of a Village Rectory

First Published in the UK in 1993 by

Spellmount Ltd
12 Dene Way
Speldhurst
Tunbridge Wells
Kent. TN3 0NX

© M. Bruce Pocklington 1993

A CIP catalogue record for this book is available from the British Library

ISBN 1-873376-03-0

Printed in Great Britain by

Biddles Ltd
Woodbridge Park
Guildford
Surrey

THE PLEASURES OF COARSE FISHING
An Angler's Pitch

By
Bruce Pocklington

SPELLMOUNT LTD
Tunbridge Wells

CONTENTS

Foreword   5

Introduction   7

One   Then and Now   11

Two   The Way Things Are   16

Three   Tackling Up For Coarse Fishing   25

Four   Groundbait, Feed And Additives   42

Five   Bait Presentation   53

Six   Float Fishing Techniques   63

Seven   A Look At Legering   81

Eight   The Quarry   88

Nine   Rod, Pole Or Perch   108

Ten   The One That Got Away   117

Eleven   Shadows On The Lake   124

Twelve   The Stream Of Life   128

Further Reading   137

Useful Adresses   138

Index   139

The drawings in this book first appeared in *Coarse Fishing Handbook* between 1984 and 1987 except for figures 1,2 and the drawing on fish identification which were drawn by Mike Reccia.

FOREWORD

How do you define a successful angler? A person with a string of huge fish to his credit? Someone prepared to sit out day and night for weeks on end in the pursuit of a particular specimen? Or maybe an inventive genius who perfects a new method or item of tackle?

A truly great angler has all of these qualities, and something else besides. And the missing ingredient is not only the most important of all but one which any angler of any degree of competence can acquire.

It is the ability to acknowledge that real success is not measured in terms of big fish on the bank, but in the pleasure obtained by the pursuit and catching of fish of whatever size or species may be available.

In more than thirty years of writing about country sports in general and fishing in particular I have not been without unfulfilled obsessions of my own. There were the big roach years, then carp and pike, then bream, and, in between, even a totally crazy period spent trying to lure a huge halibut from the depths of the Pentland Firth. As deputy editor of Angling Times and, later, editor of the Coarse Fishing Handbook (now called Coarse Fishing Today and a magazine to which Bruce has made many valuable contributions) I was not without both the opportunities and the equipment to make the captures possible. In retrospect, the missing factors were the total personal dedication and the good fortune, and my personal bream target of 8lbs was the only one I met.

Bruce's first chapter has helped me put the whole thing into its proper perspective. My personal big-fish list may be less than impressive, but no amount of money could buy the wonderful experiences involved in its compilation.

So get out there to the waterside, follow Bruce's advice, and you will certainly catch fish. Become a little obsessed with big fish if you will, but don't let that obsession rule your life. As you will discover if you follow Bruce's philosophy, the sheer pleasure of fishing for its own sake is as much fun as you will need in a lifetime.

Mike George,
Spalding, Lincolnshire.
August 1992.

ACKNOWLEDGEMENT

There have been so many influences in my angling life, some sadly no longer with us, some still wetting a line, I cannot possibly set out to thank them all individually. But I would like to say to them all collectively:

"Thanks for trying to reduce all the uncertainties in angling for me. Thanks, too, for not succeeding in that too much! You see, it is because of the uncertainties that I fish. It is also due to the aura of quiet excitement surrounding the quest, the sheer pleasure of using rod and line in natures's varying moods and the bafflement induced by elusive fish. I hope to contain fishing in my pitch, in my way, as long as I live, until my rod falls as a job lot in a car boot sale or fall into the hands of someone who loves to fish as much as I."

INTRODUCTION

This book was written with the pleasure angler in mind; that ill-defined group of anglers who are neither match men nor specialists of any kind, though they too, may find it of interest. Having said that, surely the most dedicated match men or the most assiduous seekers of specimen fish have chosen their path because of the pleasure it affords them. Yet the honing of skills, the single-mindedness of purpose and the enormous amount of time, energy and money needed to be a success in those fields would leave the average pleasure angler speechless with awe and admiration.

It is, however, the performance of the top match winner and the record breaker against which everyone else is judged and is, incidentally, against which most coarse anglers judge themselves these days.

Among the pleasure angling community there must be many who are very young or relatively inexperienced, some, perhaps, just joining our ranks, eager to find their feet. Many will be older, angling veterans of the game. I ask their indulgence if I seem to be teaching them 'how to suck eggs' in some passages. Still, I hope that they too will find something of interest within. They will know, more than most, that when it comes to angling, no-one knows everything. There is always much to learn if you have an enquiring mind and a love of nature, of which angling is so much a part.

Then there are those of varying age and circumstance who fish simply because of the pleasure it gives them. Among them are the truly addicted who never feel really content unless by river or lake they are wetting a line with maybe a fish or two to show for a day's contentment.

All are welcome to share this book with me, even the angler who airs his rod once or twice a year on family holidays, perhaps dreaming of retirement and fishing days yet to come. Yes, all are welcome to share this book with me, to identify joys and sorrows, for there is much is angling today that seems to deny it. There is a common bond between anglers of all ages, belonging, as it was, to a common tradition spanning the centuries; brotherhoods with an adherence that silently speaks of a common vocabulary, of shared techniques, of experience all know and understand and of the shared love of angling in all its variety, complexity, joy and frustration.

It is noteworthy to reflect that angling has an honorary history in the British Isles, changing with the social circumstances of the times. Dame Juliana Berners wrote on the subject in the fifteenth century, the earliest known exercise on coarse fishing. That book, the first in English, began the interesting saga of offering to the public advice and observation catching fish.

Game fishing was once the sport of the landed gentry while coarse fishing was left to the working classes. Today's angler sees the hitherto sacred class barriers breaking down while many of them choose to be unrestricted by such old notions and become 'all-round anglers', ignoring the artificial 'split' between a fish having an adipose fin or not! Even so, this book is about coarse fishing and not game, for although I have done some, it is not enough to write on the subject.

There are more women in angling than there were a few years ago, although to find one on the banks is still a cause of mild surprise. So let me make it plain; any reference to anglers automatically includes the female of the species. I really cannot bring myself to talk of fisher persons or of angling persons.

Although there are a few inalterable rules in angling and few methods and techniques that guarantee success, many articles and books give the impression that the author is the font of all angling wisdom. Some are thinly disguised advertisements of one kind or another, although there is nothing wrong with that as long as the reader recognises the fact and accepts what they deem wise, perhaps modifying to suit their own requirements and reject all else. Because of these things, in my view, a writer can only propound theories, indicate all possibilities and advise tactics.

There is very little new in fishing either. Most things are an extension or modification of older ideas. The fish hook and rod were known in ancient Egypt, for instance. Even so-called modern ideas and concepts usually thought of as being recently discovered, are but revamped ideas using modern up-to-date materials. The late Richard Walker, who could legitimately be described as innovative, collaborated with Falkus, Buller and Taylor in their book, *Successful Angling*, published by Stanley Paul of London, to point out that many examples of tackle thought to be modern were, in fact, known three centuries ago. Mind you, to emulate the chemically charged night-light we can so readily obtain, first catch your glow-worm.

There being so little new under the angler's sun, I'll break no new ground here, shake none of angling's foundations. Yet, there may be a hint, a snippet or two, a notion or concept and value still new to you, for those among you not so arrogant to learn, not too complacent or too hidebound to accept another view. You see, this book stems from my experiences, my conclusions, my theories and, yes, my emotions. Yours, more than likely, will be different. But this is my pitch - no more, no less.

Bruce Pocklington, 1993.

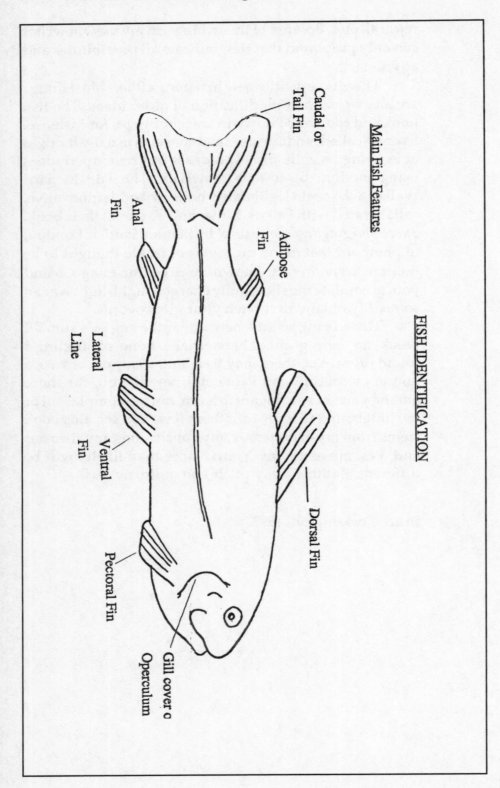

Main Fish Features

FISH IDENTIFICATION

Caudal or
Tail Fin

Anal
Fin

Adipose
Fin

Lateral
Line

Ventral
Fin

Dorsal Fin

Pectoral Fin

Gill cover o
Operculum

One

THEN AND NOW

Second World War childhood, my earliest fishing years, contained so much happiness and so much carefree living I now find it difficult to believe so much misery was being inflicted on humanity at the same time. Millions were displaced, often forever. Millions died on a world-wide scale while millions more were suffering the most horrendous torment and deprivation it is possible to inflict on fellow man.

Subsequent post-war years brought drastic changes in society. Technological advance and behavioural patterns accelerated to levels beyond those which could reasonably be expected in not less than several centuries, had not that conflict taken place.

Angling reflects something of that society so produced; and while I find much in it to applaud, there are aspects of it we could, I am sure, well do without. I am not that old but I do remember when angling was very different to what it is today. I know it is easy to view the past through rose-coloured spectacles, as older folks are prone to do, when in retrospect even the bad times are held in memory as being a hardship that could somehow prove beneficial to later generations, if only they had the opportunity to live through it.

Before today's youngsters, impatient to get at the nitty-gritty, throw this book aside as just another set of old man's tales and values, I welcome every item of tackle modern technology provides, the immense changes in standards of living and the ever wider range of opportunity now afforded older folk. However, I cannot help deploring some of the ethical and moral standards now considered normal and acceptable.

Despite tremendous material advances with attendant concepts of equality and freedom of choice, this is, in essence, a rip-off society. Its basic motivating force is a selfish one, manifesting in many anglers as a fish-at-any-cost philosophy I find repugnant. I dislike aspects of the modern scene in which those followed, idolised and emulated by the young are seen to be less that circumspect in their behaviour, flouting rules and regulations and, in some cases, breaking the law.

Fortunately, angling has yet to reach the low ebb in standards found in some other sports where drug use, cheating and the acquisition of money seems to be the motivation and the goal, even in amateur circles. Even so, rule and law breaking are prevalent in angling. It is boasted openly about, even published on occasions. It seems to be okay if you can get away with it.

Tackle stealing and the illegal removal of fish seems to be on the increase, as are selfish and anti-social attitudes commonly found by river and lake, much of which stems from that fish-at-any-cost way of life so many anglers now possess.

I find it sad too, so many anglers find their way into carp without ever having learned or experienced other forms of fishing. Many become very good carp anglers but those denied big carp by circumstance may very well be quickly disillusioned when they discover multi-rod hair rig boilies cannot bring continued success. Still, they may well have learned to handle hype, and that's something! But the saddest part for me is to see them quickly indoctrinated into a philosophy more akin to the general rat-race of work, the market place and selfish egotistical success than it ever was.

In short, in line with society, angling now seems to be based on competitive success, either as a match winner or as captor of the biggest fish. Nothing wrong with that per se, it simply reflects our competitive nature. We seem, however, to have reached a point where that kind of success is the only kind that matters, against which everything is now judged. I would have thought that life was complicated enough without taking the rat-race fishing with you.

If competitive fishing could be judged as fairly as, say, running a fixed distance or jumping a fixed height, or even as fairly as a tennis match or game of squash, I might well see some intrinsic value in it, but it cannot. Of the two, match fishing with its supervised rules and set times is by far the best assessment of individual performance but, even then, much depends on the luck of the draw, to mention the most obvious variable.

Catching the largest fish of any species, while exciting and commendable in itself, cannot, in my view, be of any value except setting the value of one angler over his contemporaries. The capture of Clarissa, the 44lb record carp, is a classic case in point. The angler, the great Dick Walker, who was lucky enough to take her, was the first to admit it was sheer chance the fish picked up his bait and not that of his companion, Pete Thomas, and modest though he was about the capture, Dick Walker was no shrinking violet. So while I can appreciate the personal, if temporary, euphoria a match win or a big fish brings to an angler, I fail to see why so many are hell bent on that kind of success, apart from the adulation it may bring or the monetary reward. Though, of course, not all are.

Many an angler hugs his success close to his chest, quietly and secretly piling up a personal record, either to keep venues and methods secret or simply to retain a kind of fishing consistent with their own philosophy, knowing that if the lid came off their exploits, their angling peace would be destroyed forever, their treasured way of life lost.

Even so, every angler hopes to fill a net or catch a whacking fish from time to time, so the angling media is almost duty bound to report such angling feats and instruct how best to emulate such performances. It keeps the accountants happy. Consequently, while many an editor might well privately dislike the way in which angling has developed in recent years and may be equally concerned for its future, a kind of self-perpetuating angling ideology has evolved for which the angling media is partly responsible.

The greater mass of anglers must involuntarily form an opinion of their own ability as being in some way lacking if they constantly match it against the selective reporting they read. It is not easy to understand, particularly for the young and inexperienced, just what personal sacrifices may have to be made to place big fish capture at the top of the successful angler's priorities. Often, very large sums of money, a massive amount of time and effort, excessive travelling, hours of preparation and hundreds of bank hours are necessary. There are attendant risks to health and normal family life. Nor are the endless days and nights of blanking usually reported. For the true specimen hunter not only sets out to catch big fish, he deliberately avoids the capture of any fish, save the largest of a particular species. These factors of specimen hunting are not usually reported. They are not newsworthy, and if they are, they are referred to lightly, skimmed over without the full implications of such fishing patterns explained.

Anyone who fishes round the clock for days on end, weeks sometimes, enduring the vagaries of the weather, living rough without catching a fish *and* travelling hundreds of miles to do it, deserves his place of honour, his fleeting hours of success and glory. To those who do it and shun all publicity, I take off my hat.

No, as you see, I am not knocking that kind of success, I admit it, providing it is done legally, but for me my order of life's priorities *puts the enjoyment of fishing itself before size or number of fish*. That is how I was taught to regard coarse fishing and that is how I have tried to continue throughout my life. I say try, because the pressures of the rat-race in angling, as I have unkindly put it, are ever present.

I recognised the futility of the big fish syndrome as soon as I had caught my first twenty-pounder, a carp. Until that day, (night actually) I admit to a slight attack of the neurotics, feeling incomplete as an angler somehow. Silly, I know, but there it is. I'd had a nineteen-pounder a long time before the twenty came, that's the real stupidity of it, the lesser fish being much harder to induce to take and much more ferocious in its struggle not to be landed. I realised smaller fish were often equally hard to catch, often fought better and certainly gave as much pleasure.

How about a thirty or forty pounder? I saw, too, that from where I happen to live it would take a disproportionate amount of time, effort and money to be in with a chance of picking one up. As far as I'm concerned it's just not worth the hassle.

Two

THE WAY THINGS ARE

This chapter looks at the problems within angling today. The sheer number of people now fishing has intensified the demand for fishable waters and as waters disappear forever, victims of urban expansion, and as many rivers, streams, drains and canals have had their nature changed due to public demand for more and more water, the cheaper the better, such waterways suffering from abstraction or the results of irrigation and drainage engineering, in some cases being denuded of natural life until they have become clear, straight almost sterile water channels, so have anglers' demands increased until they are now at a premium.

Offsetting the decline to some extent, gains have been made in the maturing of gravel pits, sand pits and the like since the war.

Fortunately, in very recent years, water engineers have managed to strike a better compromise between the conflicting demands imposed on waterways and the arrival of a 'greener' society. Society offers hope that the future of beautiful rivers and other waters will retain their natural function as well as continuing to supply the public priority for clean water with adequate irrigation and drainage. However, the fight against pollution continues in the courts.

As traditional barriers between game and coarse fishing are falling, with many anglers now enjoying both, as much but not all applies to coarse and game anglers alike. The increase in purpose-made lakes now caters for both factions too. If the sea angler encounters problems of litter and oil slicks, the solution may be international. It will almost certainly be political! So, on the whole, every angler will find something here with which he can identify.

Fish Stealing

The illegal removal of fish from one water to another is not now unknown in coarse fishing. Once more or less confined to the use of live bait for pike, it now includes the removal of larger fish. The traditional salmon poacher's spoils were intended to grace someone's table but today's thief is much more likely to take very large carp, the aim being to enhance one water at the expense of another. For all I know money may change hands but, more likely, such a selfish act is committed simply to improve fishing, big carp now being at a premium and attracting anglers from far and wide. The theft is not only illegal, it is carried out against fellow anglers who, having paid their dues will carry on fishing for stock no longer there. Unless fish stocks are carefully vetted by qualified authorities there is the attendant risk of spreading disease and wiping out fish stocks, a propensity nature has without anglers lending a helping hand.

Pollution

Anglers usually define pollution as being the poisoning of waters by the introduction of toxic substances. I regard pollution as being more than that. The contamination of the environment with litter and discarded rubbish also constitutes pollution, in my view. Such rubbish as is left by freshwater not only detracts from the natural beauty of the scene, it constitutes a threat to the safety of farm stock and wildlife, causing severe injury and often death. Various forms, such as plastic bottles and discarded line are the main dangers, such substances are not always biodegradable. Empty tins will rust away eventually but it takes a long time, bringing the dangers of damaged feet and cut mouths to cattle and sheep. Anglers, or anyone else, come to that, who leaves litter and rubbish of any kind to defile the environment are also a threat to angling's future.

Public Reaction

The British public can hardly be described as litter conscious and their knowledge of angling is limited. Most of them do not even know that coarse anglers return fish to the water unharmed. The number of times I have explained to members of the public our procedure, that we do not 'throw them back' nor eat them, but carefully return them to their environment, is staggering. To many of them, we are lumped together with their image of game fishing, particularly salmon. Yet I believe we shall need their support in the future. Law breaking is news and attracts wide publicity while littered banks will hardly create an image of 'caring' anglers. Those who break the law and leave litter, which is unsightly and often dangerous are providing ammunition for those who seek to ban angling as being a cruel anti-social pastime.

The Law

Those among us who scorn the law tend to forget it is the law that gives us the right to fish at all, as well as protecting our access to water. Laws can be changed. The rights we hold can be taken away. So it's not just a matter of being holier than thou, it's a matter of angling's survival. On that count alone, it behoves us to keep the law and follow local rules and regulations, no matter how stupid they may seem. Laws are changed by private or public pressure and are retained by the same means. There are enough anglers with vested interests to ensure our public image is a good one, if every angler works towards that end. Whatever your political allegiance may be, your representative should be in no doubt that your vote depends on his or her support of angling.

The Benefits of Angling

It is difficult to express to a non-angler just why people fish at all. Apart from appealing to the intellect, the pursuit of fish requires an analytical mind and constructive thinking, it provides opportunity to observe at first hand nature, to exercise certain skills and learning what is usually defined as watercraft; that is reading certain signs and deducing from them fish behaviour, a more difficult task than people imagine. It provides exercise for our competitive nature without recourse to extremes of violence often associated with other sports and, of course, it supports a million pound industry with the subsequent staffing possibilities.

It is also educational and the angler becomes 'green' and something of a naturalist. Perhaps what is more important, it offers relief from stress and life's pressures. It is eminently therapeutic. These things are patently obvious to the angler.

There is, it is suggested by some, a much deeper reason, the fish and its capture being something of man's history, a basic trait buried in the genes of Man. Whether that is so or not, I don't know. What I do know is its capacity for lifting the spirit! It is said that more people - with a growing number of females among them - participating in the sport more than all the others, as opposed to being an indolent spectator that is, make the sport one of the most popular. That is a thought political representatives would do well to remember.

Admittedly, there is within our ranks a minority of uncaring, law and rule breaking litter louts, their behaviour, as in all other activities, creating a yardstick against which we are all judged, providing an image we could well do without. They are our worst enemies.

Caring for the Quarry

I will never be convinced that a fish feels pain from a hook in the lips. Likewise, I would take a lot of convincing they are never hurt or damaged by some anglers, never mind the trauma they go through when being caught, tethered to a line, hauled out of their environment and subjected to prolonged exposure to the air. The hook can be no more painful than the food and debris they constantly examine by sucking in, testing and blowing out again. Finding food they suck it in, crush it in pharyngeal teeth and swallow it. In go bits of stick, stones, caddis-fly cases, seeds, oysters, crustaceans of all types, crayfish, sticklebacks, small perch and other fry - all of which have less than harmless spiny fins, most fish being cannibalistic for at least part of their lives. It is actually possible to set the hook in their mouths without them knowing it, without them showing any reaction at all. I've done it! Once they feel the line, however, they panic, feel tethered, even if the experience is new to them. If the feeling is NOT new to them, they panic still more because the out-of-water experience is terrifying. There is actually a theory in some carping circles that some carp are prepared to be caught, the 'reward' being a tasty and nourishing piece of food. I think that is pushing human intelligence or fish interpretation too far! In carping fish terms, they are 'mug' fish!

Fortunately for anglers, fish have small brains, little intellect and short memories. If that were not so, they would never be caught at all!

The trauma of being caught has little to do with hook penetration, but starts in the split second the line is felt and ends as the fish re-enters the water, having been played in to the landing net, transferred from there to keepnet or sack, held there indefinitely with up to hordes of others, perhaps weighed and photographed and put back into the water. Such trauma lasts anything from a few minutes to many hours. It seems patently obvious that the next subject I wish to consider and I hope convince you is that it is down to us all to reduce the trauma as much as possible and give no-one a chance to label us cruel and selfish.

Minimising Trauma

The fact is that a great deal can be done to reduce the stress of a fish being caught; some of it easily achieved, some of it contentious to say the least. Imagine the indignant furore a keepnet ban would cause! Such bans have been used on private waters and the evidence points towards healthier fish and improved fishing. The modern, knotless meshes are vast improvements on the old types with their smoother profile and their generous proportions, but can you honestly say you have never found loose scales or fish slime in them after the net has been emptied? Once the protective mucus and scales have been lost a fish becomes defenceless against the invasion of parasites and other diseases. Even in modern nets some fish tend to snag their dorsal fins, tearing them and the net. Barbel and carp have a tendency to do this. Keepsacks of softer, smoother material with innumerable perforations are used and only then one fish at a time. The ensuing darkness helps to keep them quiet and still, but even then there are risks in the use of nets and sacks if used improperly.

Retention

Every angler loves to retain fish until the end of a session to record weight of catch, photograph it, or simply to look at! It's part of the game, especially match fishing. However, to minimise the trauma to fish, nets and sacks should be thoroughly wetted before use and should not be overcrowded. The good angler has more than one net or sack to hand should it prove necessary to use them. Large weights of fish stuffed into a keepnet damage each in their attempts to find oxygen and escape, so it should be placed in deep water where it will be cooler. Consequently, the water will contain more oxygen. It's even more important to place keepsacks containing large fish, making sure the sack is firmly attached to the bank. As far as is possible, especially in running water, a net, whether it is designed for single, large fish or otherwise, is best secured parallel to the bank, the fish with its head upstream. The carpsack is best off with one corner cut off, leaving a hole large enough to allow the carp's mouth to protrude through it, but not so large as to uncover the eyes. That way the fish gets more oxygen while being quiet. One other odd use of the keepnet, in my opinion, is to stake it out in a fast, relatively shallow flow of water. Water may well cover the fish, but to keep them swimming with no respite from the main steam is like having a hamster in a treadwheel with no possible escape!

In any kind of fishing other than match fishing it is best to have weighing and photographing equipment ready to hand, not forgetting to wet hands and weigh sling before either come into contact with the fish. A quick wetting of the hands will suffice to protect fish from the heat of hands that will feel like a burn to a cold-blooded fish. Fish of any size should not be subjected to anything other than a soft, preferably wet, material on which they are often unhooked. Most places have a soft, grassy area. Big fish may need re-wetting while being photographed. It helps the fish and enhances the photograph. Keep your catch low to the ground and support it along its length and be ready at all times to anticipate a wriggle that could have it out of your hands in a second. Hands up how many anglers have never dropped a fish?

So until better alternative means of fish retention are found, the only thing to do, if we must retain them at all, is to keep their imprisonment as short and as comfortable as possible to minimise their stress.

Unhooking

Never fish without having a disgorger at hand. The cheap plastic ones are fine. They are brightly coloured and easy to find when dropped.

They also float! For bigger fish and bigger hooks use a pair of surgical forceps. I own a pair with long, curved ends and a shorter, straight pair. For pike trebles a 17-inch pike disgorger by Drennan I find useful. With those four disgorgers every hook and every fish is recovered. I know barbless hooks are less harmful but I'm never completely happy using them. Unless a water's rules insist on their use the farthest I will go is to flatten the barb or use semi-barbed hooks. Little harm is done to the fish by the barb going in, the damage is done by the barb being hastily removed in my experience. If the hook resists removal to any great degree I cut the line close to the hook and remove the hook, bend first. Proper care in hook removal leaves but a tiny hole that heals up. If the hook is too far down the throat, better snip the line as close to the hook as possible, leaving it in rather than tear the fish trying to get it out. Fish have a remarkable ability to shed hooks quickly. Indeed, some fish have the ability to get rid of the hook while being played. Tench have been known to dive to a snag and leave the hook there. Carp, too, head straight for known snags, but if they can get there they do not seem to have the same ability as tench, and it can be said they do not have the same ability to escape. It is far more likely to tether itself to the snag by getting the bomb entangled. Where such problems are envisaged with any fish when legering use a bomb-link weaker than the main line or a semi-fixed bomb that comes away under stress, reducing the chances of the fish becoming exhausted in attempting to get free. Better still, if it is safe to do so, go in and release the fish yourself, although I would not suggest you do it at night or if you are on your own. For those occasions when it is difficult to find soft ground on which to lay your fish, the use of an unhooking mat is recommended.

If all the above seems a great trouble to take I can only say I believe it to be good angling practice and correct in that if we are not seen as being careful and considerate in the way we handle fish, again, we are giving ammunition to the anti-angling pressures in our society.

I have no hesitation in repeating the message I am trying to get across. *Unless we determine to be law-abiding, anti-polutionists who care for the welfare of our quarry, we shall be branded as being the opposite of that; moronic, cruel, litter louts not averse to rule, regulation and law breaking when it suits us!*

Who wants that description? Certainly not I!

Important Note:

Apart from foiling attempts by anti-anglers to stick unfair labels on us, there is a very good reason for every angler to reduce fish stress as much as possible. The less stress, the easier it is to catch fish again! The more stress imposed on fish stocks, the more difficult successful angling becomes for everyone.

Three

TACKLING UP FOR COARSE FISHING

The tackle trade overall is big business and is very competitive, offering the angler keen prices, tackle development and innovation with an ever growing range of goods. The local retailer and the mail order firm are the two main sources of supply, each with advantages over the other, dependent in both cases on the size of the operation.

The Local Retailer

Few retailers develop such a relationship as exists between shop and angler, not dissimilar to the once popular general store corner shop in which one would be treated as a valued customer; a place where idiosyncratic needs were seen to and as such shops once dispensed local gossip, so does the tackle shop provide much more than material goods. In my view, a tackle shop should be chosen with as much care as swim and fishing venues are selected, for the best of them are run by people who provide a fund of information, have an ear to the grapevine and will dispense it freely, including advice which can be invaluable, faced as we are by such an enormous range of tackle to deal with. It's as well to remember, however, a dealer is there to make a living. No matter how friendly, informative and basically honest the best of them might be, they are unlikely to turn away business to customers who do not ask for advice or ignore it when offered. It is of little use going into a shop at peak trading times and expecting undivided and lengthy attention, however. Choose less busy times to do business, if you can. Leave the purchase of important and costly items until you can shop at leisure.

Many tackle shops are just too small to stock a full range of game, sea and coarse tackle, along with respective clothing, so if you are in a small minority of his customers it may not be a viable proposition for the shop to stock your requirements.

Despite their good intentions, retailers are sometimes let down by suppliers or wholesalers, even with nationally advertised goods in the weeks leading up to a new season. Your friendly, local tackle shop may well-run local matches, have credit free 'saving' schemes and offer such services as tackle repair, video rental and invariably bait supply. Indeed, such shops often build up a reputation for the quality of their bait and its availability while it is not unknown for a shop to go under because the demand for bait declines, thus losing valuable customers.

In assessing tackle shops, many anglers consider the quality of bait and the advice available to be more important than tackle availability. After all, you need good bait on a week to week basis while good tackle can be acquired almost anywhere and major items such as rods, reels and tackle boxes, etc. are required not that often! In my view, the honest, friendly knowledgeable proprietor is likely to give discount as a regular customer; those which give excellent bait service and other supplementary services deserve, and should get, all the support you can give. If he goes down and shuts shop, it is angling's loss and not just yours.

Mail Order

Brochures published annually by such firms are well worth acquiring, even if they cost a quid or two. Not only are they informative, interesting and comprehensive, they are sometimes very amusing. I have to say I have never personally experienced any dissatisfaction in dealing with them, even though goods are bought unseen, although there is the dissatisfaction of paying packing and postal charges. They usually offer standard credit facilities and it is from them you can usually buy items not freely available in your area, especially if you tend to specialise in your coarse fishing. I've always found them fair in their dealings, which is more than can be said for some tackle shops I've entered in my time! A word of warning; rip-off merchants exist in the tackle business just as in other trade. Let the buyer beware!

ROD ACTION AND TEST CURVE RATING

Fig.1, below, shows how rods are built with different actions, dependent on their intended purpose. The tip-action rod at (A) is, for example, the type used as a match or float rod, meant to be flexible at the tip, casting relatively light weights, yet stiffening quickly towards the butt, to pick up line off the water quickly; all of which is ideal for responding speedily to the dip of a float and maintaining efficient line control. Other rods may have similar or slightly longer tip action while having a greater test curve, as in (B), thus being able to cast heavier weights.

Below: Fig.1. Rod Action

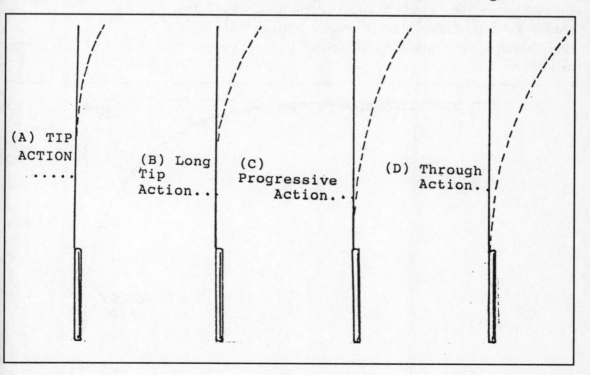

(A) TIP ACTION
.....

(B) Long Tip Action..

(C) Progressive Action..

(D) Through Action.

Description of a rod is given by a simple code with, say, A, B, C and D, describing actions as in Fig.1, with the addition of a number that indicates the weight it was made to cast, ie A12 or C40, the casting weight being in grams.

The Test Curve Rating

Many rods are still described by their test curve rating; the weight in pounds required to pull the tip end down until it is as right angles with the butt, ie ¾lb TC, 1½lb TC, 2lb TC, 2½lb TC and so on. These figures indicate the maximum weight in ounces the rod was designed to cast.

It was an accurate measure of a rod's capabilities when the rod materials were glass fibre, but it is less accurate with the more modern carbon and composites. Even so, it is still widely used today. The angler need not be duly concerned, the modern rods, often computer designed, more than compensate for the loss of glass fibre characteristics, and both the test curve and the action of the rod give a good guide to a rod's capabilities. Both are shown here to define the difference between the two, there being some confusion, I've found, in some people's minds.

Below: Fig.2. Test Curve Rating

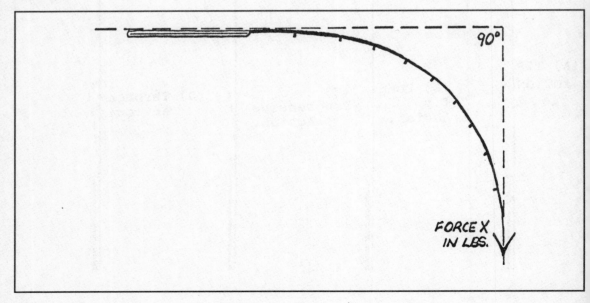

Choosing a Rod

Before entering a shop with rod purchase in mind, or pole come to that, it is assumed from catalogues, brochures and such, you have some idea of what you want. Listening to other anglers can be a help but bear in mind few people admit to having bought a pup. Better still, if you can borrow one of the same model, even if only for a few minutes, it will tell you more than all you may read or hear on the subject, especially if it is used in similar circumstances to your own angling, for your own fishing style may be different from that of another. The overriding factor in choice may be the cost and money can be saved by buying part-built rods, particularly if you are good at do-it-yourself kinds of work. It also provides the opportunity of building a rod entirely to your specifications. If you cannot borrow a rod to try out, at least fit your reel to get the set-up, to get the feel of it, as its balance, or lack of it, can be very important. If spot on, it can be held in one hand for hours, if necessary, without undue strain. If not, it can become less than pleasurable in use and, thus, less efficient.

Mass produced tackle has been designed for the average angler, no doubt, so if you have anything but average dimensions - short fingers, long forearms, for instance - the ideal, ready-made rod may not exist. In theory, with the reel secured as high up the butt as it can be fitted, the butt itself should protrude no more than about two inches below the elbow, while the angler should be able to drop his forefinger to the spool rim when the rod is held at the spool and the rod should be in balance at that point. With the float rod, or any rod hand-held for long periods, the feel of balance is very important, the rod becoming an extension of the forearm. With leger rods, spending most of their time in rod rests, it is far less so. If the rod is butt heavy, pulling back the reel may do the trick. If ring heavy, and rings are deceptively so, a piece of lead inserted in the butt should help balance it.

Modern carbon and composite rods are a great deal lighter than older thick-walled glass fibre ones, so total weight is less of a problem. I don't know if I'm a biological freak but I always have to compromise reel positions on most rods. Look for a butt diameter that is neither too thick nor too thin, or strain will assuredly develop in the hand or fingers.

Ring spacing and their number causes dissent among anglers, as few agree on such matters. No-one can deny, however, that the more rings employed, the greater the line friction caused and that the fewer used the less the line follows the smooth arc of a bent rod. All rods are a compromise between various factors, none more so than ring spacing which undoubtedly affects casting distance and butt-end indication sensitivity. Whether rings are lined or not, in my view, both tip and butt-end rings should both be lined on every rod, bearing the brunt of wear and tear as they do, is a matter for conjecture. Lined rings certainly dissipate heat quickly and it is difficult to determine how many lines are worn or part, due solely to heat.

Modern rod-making materials have certainly improved rod efficiency in terms of weight, casting ability and watertightness at least. They can be made longer and thinner whilst retaining strength to accept casting weight and have enough flexibility to deal with fighting fish. Many an older angler, while welcoming the modern rod materials, might well rue the sacrifices made to the sheer pleasure of playing a fish on glass fibre. For many, such pleasure is difficult to recapture on ultra-modern carbons. Irrespective of its make up or materials, any rod had to be a compromise between a casting tool and the playing of fish at close quarters. In float rods the compromise in not that important, the criteria being in picking line off the water quickly while retaining flexibility at tip end is conducive to handling fish carefully. In leger fishing, long range rods, the factors are more extreme. A rod without enough 'punch' to cast heavy bombs well over a hundred yards may prove less than ideal for handling big fish in the margins.

There are limits to everyone's financial resources and while a Utopian dream for anglers would be to own the perfect rod for every situation, reality really dictates that most of us have to compromise, making do with what we have. For those happy to fish in consistently similar circumstances, two or three rods may suffice. For those of us who do fish a wide variety of rivers and stillwaters, for a variety of fish, their rod collection, like Alice, will grow and grow.

Most mass produced rods are marketed for the taste or susceptibility of a broad spectrum of the angling scene with limited inroads into the specialist areas of fishing. Similarly, smaller firms, even one-man enterprises, are more likely to come up with rods for a particular purpose within specialist fields. If, as a pleasure angler, you find yourself more and more interested in what could be termed a specialist approach, you'll find the rod of your dreams available among the many advertised in specialist literature. The latter are more likely to offer the right rod, to your specifications, albeit at a higher price, particularly if they are endorsed by a famous name.

Essentially a tube, rods tend to be oval in cross-section when curved. Manufacturers claim several ploys to offset this fact. It is sometimes an advantage to note qualities not claimed for a rod because this often leads to an indication of any inherent deficiency in its make-up. It's also true that a rod from the top end of a composite may be better than the cheaper carbon. Unless when buying a rod you follow advertising hype like a sheep, the sheer number available and the seemingly conflicting criteria by which they are described, can make it all very confusing indeed.

Martin James, the BBC broadcaster, expressed the idea to me that it was a pity the boron and carbon ranges swept away the glass fibre rods before development had reached its limit. I'm sure he's right!

Finally on rods, the type is a function of length, taper, action and wall thickness and diameter. Watch out for any 'flat spots' in the rod's curve, often caused by badly applied rings, or rings with unsuitable feet. It's rarely due to the manufacture of the blank.

Examination of a few rods will immidiately make it apparent which have good, bad or indifferent finishes.

The quality of rings, whippings, reel seating, butt materials and varnishing add or subtract from the rod's appearance, its useful life and durability over time in terms of efficiency. Flashy rods have no place over easily spooked fish; quiet colours are more appropriate. Beware, however, the poor blank hidden beneath certain quality and just remember everything on a rod can be changed later - except the all important blank.

Buying a Reel

Once you have a reel, unless you have access to a good engineering works, you are more or less stuck with it. Its price will reflect the quality more than you think. Cheaper reels, apparently of good quality, will have, almost certainly, inferior design and engineering standards and materials therein and thereupon. Despite its workload, a good reel, given regular servicing and reasonable treatment, will last for many years. A bad reel may pack up within the first season of use. Comments herein are restricted to the popular fixed spool reel because most anglers never use a centre-pin or multiplier reel these days.

The Fixed Spool Reel

A reel takes an awful hammering in its life, revolving an incredible amount of times, its mechanism subject to strain and is often subjected to less than careful treatment in use and transportation. Its actual working life is spent in close proximity to water, mud and grit, as well as operating in all weathers. Prime requisites are, then, that it has good engineering standards and be watertight. The space age materials now used in construction certainly suffer less from the ravages of corrosion than from the latter-day counterparts, but they tend, I find, to attract dirt and dust, breadcrumbs, etc. more easily. Some versions also have dodgy assembly methods such as cover plates fixed with self-tapping screws, biting into the woodwork itself without a bush, washer or nut. This may be fine in the early days but unless great care is used when servicing, it could well lead to problems. Modern graphite reels will balance more easily on modern rods and will add less weight to an otherwise light carbon than many older models.

Despite my grumbles, we are spoilt for choice with rods, many offering features, and selling on the strength of them. I find this distracts men from the essential function I look for. For legering work I prefer a skirted spool and a rear drag control clutch that once it is set I can trust, despite changes in temperature and humidity. An easily replaceable spool is for me, with a push-button release, far better than a clutch retained by a screw, incorporating clutch release.

All the control I want should be ergonomically situated to suit my style of legering, which includes playing a fish off the clutch. I like the handle to be ambidextrously mounted, securable when it is mounted by a screw-top locking device (I've had a reel with a push-button type of handle locking device, the handle of which collapsed under pressure in use).

A good strong bail arm that requires a moderate pressure to close it when turning the handle, rather than snapping shut almost of its own accord by the impetus of casting is another factor I look for. The bail arm must have a freely moving line-guide roller without end play, in which line can be trapped and damaged - a point to watch for in all reels, whatever their intended use.

The external reel profile needs to be such as to avoid catching line loops while, internally, the gearing between handle and spool ought to be of a quality that has no appreciable backlash in its assembly, at least not enough to cause concern. As I leger a great deal using butt indication methods, I need reels that allow easy bobbin adjustments and quick 'locking' when the rod is taken up and the bail is closed by turning the handle. In short, I look for reels with as many anti-reverse positions as possible. A great deal is made of ball bearing usage in construction by manufacturers but I've known reels to be too easily rotated in setting up for legering, the carrier head and handle turning of their own accord. Providing a reel has most of the qualities I seek, I am not at all that concerned whether the carrier head spins true. Better if it does though but, to me, it's not a disaster.

The Abu Cardinal, the fifty-fives I have cover most of the main facts I have mentioned, although later models have only one reverse position. I also own a pair of Shimano bait-runners that neatly avoid many of the minor, niggly inconveniences of the Cardinal, allowing a quick bobbin setting and adjustment, although that is not their main advantage of course. The bait-runner system, originally designed for the American market, but neatly adapted for the legering methods here, is no longer available only from Shimano. This runner system, in operation by activating a switch, is immediately overridden by turning the reel handle, to bring the more normal clutch into operation. The bait-runner simply allows line to be drawn off with a closed bail arm under varying degrees of resistance from nil upwards. I find the anti-reverse switch fiddly, but other than that it is a well-built reel. Its graphite body attracts and accumulates dirt easily, but you should by now be getting the idea. It is unlikely that any reel has every feature on it that you require.

For float fishing, I have Mitchell reels, mainly because of their quality and smoothness in operation. The Mitchells are much better than most in regard to their line-laying qualities too, a factor I find more important with fine lines and shallow spools, though many anglers would argue that for really long distance casting, the reverse is true. I rarely fish where it is necessary to cast beyond ninety yards or so, a distance easily reached without recourse to the finer points of long-range casting. Other choices to make and watch out for are spool dimensions, which includes line capacity and the availability of spare spools. Sometimes all spares are extra and sometimes they are included in the reel's buying price.

Fishing is a relaxed affair for me. Nothing, in my view, is gained by hustle and bustle, including line retrieval. Speed for speed's sake leads to inefficiency. Even a match angler, keen not to waste a second of his time, might well introduce inaccuracy if there is a sense of hurried anxiety about his actions. That being so, I see little need for gearing ratios much in excess of about 4:1.

Further tips to note

Some reels lay line profiles anything but level. If they slope to the back of the spool, line flow is hampered, while if they slope to the spool rim, line can spin off too easily. The worst are those with a 'hump' in the middle. Much depends on how the line is loaded, the correct use of backing line, if used, as well as the inherent line-laying qualities of the reel itself. When loading the spool try to make sure the line leaves the spool in the same direction as the carrier head rotation and try to apply an even pressure to the line without it biting into or leaving loose coils here and there. A minor point is the provision of a line clip on the spool. I do have reels without a line clip, due to their other more different features, but it's still a source of annoyance to resort to separate line retaining clips or elastic bands to prevent line spillage in storing or in transit. Keep your reel clean and free from grit, especially from areas where ingress is likely, and watch out for a build-up of dirt on the spool rim which can reduce line flow on the cast. If you acquire spare spools, sticking a small label indicating the line's breaking strain to an inconspicuous part of the spool is a good idea, lest you forget, like me, what they are.

Line Matters

Of the three types of line normally available, namely braided, multi-strand and monofilament, the latter reigns supreme as a main line in coarse fishing. Braided line has in the past been restricted to hook length due to its softer more supple qualities, often necessary in the search for big fish. In turn this has quickly been overtaken by multistrand in the endless search for innovative measures to outwit the denizens of the deep. Braided and multistrand require a different approach by anglers, in terms of knotting and even complete rigs.

Any angler old enough to have fished with catgut or silk lines will agree the innovation and development of monofilament line has done more to advance catch rates in coarse fishing than any other factor. The mono line is so reliable and is of such consistency over its whole length, it is almost taken for granted. It's true, its strength and consistency of diameter are remarkable considering the thousands of miles of the stuff made each year. However, we should remain alert to the fact that somewhere along its length it is still possible, though unlikely, that there is a flaw resulting in a weak spot. Such weaknesses can only increase with time and in use, sunlight being the major threat - and of course wear and tear alone may cause line failure eventually. Different lines have an in-built degree of 'elasticity' or stretch. Some are sold as pre-stretched, being finer, of less diameter for a given breaking strain. These have a tendency towards being more brittle, a fact to bear in mind fishing near snags, over sharp bars, encrusted with stones or mussel shells etc. I think it is fair to say, unless you are an experienced angler, avoid pre-stretched line until you have at least some angling experience.

Few of us know how old line is before it arrives in the shop, but no-one need buy line that is stored in the wrong manner. It should never be stored near heat not exposed to sunlight as both of these can cause deterioration by affecting molecular cohesion in the line. It works out cheaper to buy bulk line and no storekeeper should refuse you a quick line test, if you ask. It may only be valid for the piece of line you pull off the end of the spool, but if you are perceived as being fussy, perhaps knowledgeable, you are much less likely to be offered duff goods of any kind, let alone line he knows to be suspect. If the line breaks well below its stated breaking strain, don't buy it! Incidentally, braided line always does, but should not be discarded because of that. That's the normal state of things; it's made to standards acceptable to the American market. Line is cheap enough to be replaced quite frequently. If it receives heavy usage or is subject to pulling for a break, gets snagged up, or has been given excessive strain, renew it, thus removing any doubts about its condition. If kinks or flats have been formed in the line again, renew it. Such imperfections can often be seen but are revealed by running the line through the fingertips, or even the mouth, when a small anomaly will be very evident.

Choosing

Choosing a line is a very important thing. Most anglers try many lines before gaining a liking for a particular line. For myself, I find lines up to above 3lbs in the Shakespeare Omni range suitable. From 3lbs to about 7lbs I like Maxima or Drennan Specimen lines, while from 7lbs to 15lbs I like Sylcast Sorrel. Your choice may be different. If you are happy with your choice we shall both be right.

Some lines have more memory than others, retaining the spiral as they come off the spool, lying along the bottom like a coiled spring in the worst cases. It's also worth noting that line, even that claimed to be invisible, attract microscopic dust particles to themselves in water which in sunlight, viewed from below, sticks out like a sore thumb. If anything at all spells danger to a wary fish, that will, though there is not a lot you can do about it. Perhaps one of the criteria which causes a line to appeal to an angler is the ease with which knots are formed in it.

Knotty Problems

The tying of knots undoubtedly weakens monofilament lines. The wet knot strength of a line can be remarkably lower than its standard breaking strain. Much of the strength lost in tying knots can be regained by first, always lubricating a knot with your own spit before it is tightened. Second, by careful formation of the knot and third, by using a suitable knot for the job in hand. Against that, there has to be considered cold hands and fingers, dim or dark conditions when fishing and knot damage when in use, especially from legering rigs. Nothing is worse than losing a fish because of knot failure, so it is worth taking the trouble to try and eliminate the possibility, even if it means learning new knots or repeatedly tying in multi-strand lines, its form allowing the noose end to be trimmed off close. The double grinner is a superb knot for joining two lines together. It is more fussy to tie than the knots until, at a pinch, you can do it blindfold!

Below: Fig.3. The Grinner Knot

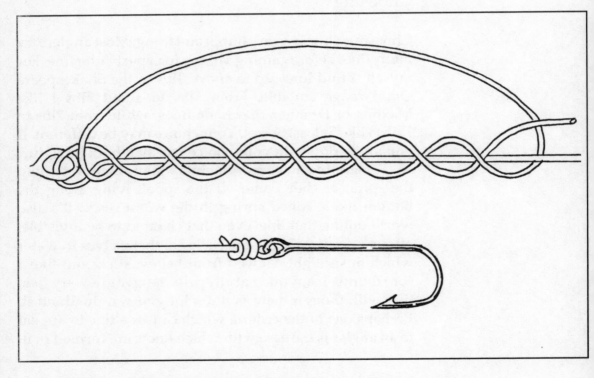

Figs.3-7 show the knots I tend to use the most, having found them to be reliable and easy to tie. Because much of my fishing demands the use of swivels and eye hooks, I use the grinner knot more than any other, its quality residing in the fact that it forms a noose, the turns of which draw tighter as pressure is applied without strangling the knot by cutting into any of the turns or any sort of tuck. It is a neat knot and can be employed in mono and, with care,

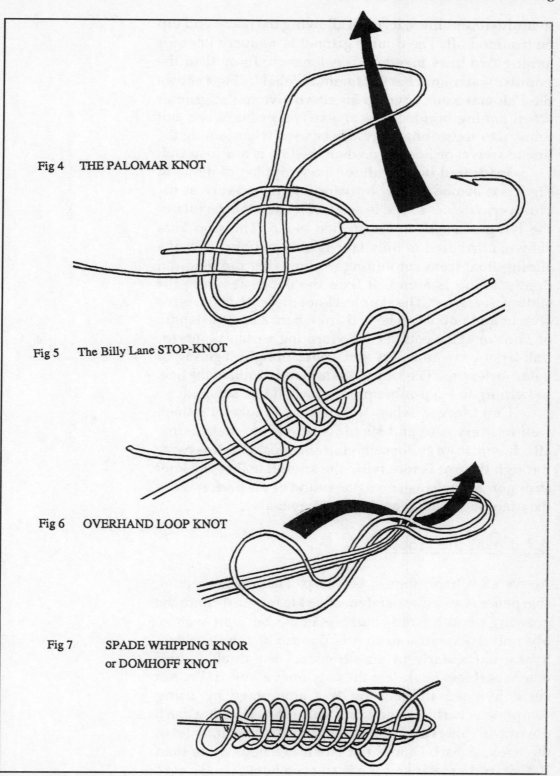

Fig 4   THE PALOMAR KNOT

Fig 5   The Billy Lane STOP-KNOT

Fig 6   OVERHAND LOOP KNOT

Fig 7   SPADE WHIPPING KNOR
or DOMHOFF KNOT

in multi-strand lines, its form allowing the noose end top be trimmed off. The double grinner is a superb knot for joining two lines together. It is far more fussy than the popular water knot but it is far more reliable. Fig.4 shows the Palomar knot, used as an alternative to the grinner when joining braided line to a swivel or hook eye, but remember the grinner may also be used when joining the line to swivel or hook eye when the line is multi-strand.

Spade end hooks call for the whipping of mono in Fig.7, a task made easier by using a tying aid such as the Huktyer, a device found in any tackle shop that facilitates the tying of small hooks to fine mono. The stop knot shown, attributed to Billy lane is used only to prevent a sliding float from continuing to slide after the required depth setting is found. It fixes the depth at which the sliding float is set. The simplest knot presented here is the Overhand knot. It can be tied anywhere along the length of a line or at the end, the loop forming anchor points for link legers, swimfeeders and hooks in light legering or paternoster rigs. The loop tends to stand proud of the line, so helping to keep subsequent attached line separate.

Don't forget, when tying knots, to lubricate them well in every case and should you wish to make a line attachment to an eye or swivel stronger pass the line twice through the eye before tying the knot. It makes the knot stronger. In such instances, the round eye is preferable to the diamond shaped eyes that are available.

A Look at the Hook

Above all a hook should be sharp. That means a hook sharpener is an essential item of tackle for me despite the growing trend towards barbless hooks on some waters. My only concession to that is the use of semi-barbless hooks, particularly in pike trebles. I use doubles, and where barbless hooks are the only ones allowed. I'm not yet convinced there is no less advantage by using completely barbless though I will often flatten a barb down with pliers and fish happily with just a hump let in the hook. A barb should not bite into a hook more than 10% of its diameter and if it is an eyed hook, I make sure the eye is fully closed without any abberation that could damage line. I have used every conceivable hook pattern on the market, even those with the barb on the outside of the bend. I still remain faithful to some old favourites, even though I collect hooks in the way many anglers collect floats! From size 6 to size 2, for my money the Au Lion D'or takes some beating. The size 6 in particular seems to screw itself in, even tough it is in-pointed and requires a touch of the whetstone now and again to keep it sharp. Au Lion D'or hooks are forged and are very strong. From size 6 to size 14 I go for Drennan Specialist Hooks or the chemically sharpened Kamasans, while hooks smaller than that I'm not at all bothered who makes them, to be honest. I rarely fish with anything less than a 20, in any case, not being a dyed-in-the-wool caster and maggot fisher. No doubt those who do fish regularly with such minute hooks would say it matters a great deal who makes them and what pattern they are. Only the other week I was fishing for 'bits' deliberately on a hard-fished water alongside an obviously experienced match angler. He took about thirty fish in the time it took me to struggle for two. We were, in fact, quiver tipping red maggot, each of us using groundbait on occasions. I began to think that some of my hook sizes were at fault, as well as my bankside demeanour, because he talked incessantly in a loud voice, literally shouting in triumph as each wriggling victim was swung towards the bank. Some five days later, by sheer chance, we were both again on the same water. I could not stop catching fish; he had none. The roles were reversed. After two hours on the float without a bite, he changed to quivertip paternostering, the means by which I was enjoying success. He began to catch. Where do you go on such conflicting evidence? Such are the imponderables of angling!

Hooks are mass produced, and with the larger sizes at least, it is worthwhile testing each for temper before use. If you don't you may live to regret it...as I did.

Four

GROUNDBAIT, FEED AND ADDITIVES

Propriety groundbait mixers of many types are almost universally available from tackle shops. Their special characteristics and uses are clearly explained on the package along with mixing directives that should be meticulously followed to get the best out of them. Like all convenience products, they tend to be expensive but a proportion of their individual attractive properties can be incorporated into a basic breadcrumb mix giving 'life' to an otherwise prosaic mix.

Basic Crumb Mixes

White and brown breadcrumb powders are also widely available and can suffice for most angling situations. White crumb has better binding situations than brown, although each can be used on its own. More usually, the two are mixed in various proportions.

As bought, though usually pure, on rare occasions they need to be put through a household sieve to remove lumps and impurities. When mixing the two together, a good and quick method to ensure a thorough mix is to put the powders into a plastic bag, seal the neck and agitate the bag for a few minutes. You will require to buy about four times as much brown as white. Store them in dry, mouse-proof containers. I can find large screw-type containers, such as plastic sweet bottles useful for this purpose, though to keep larger quantities you may have to resort to plastic buckets with snap lids, or even larger bins.

Mixing

Many anglers claim the best mixes are made by addition of water from the swim you are about to fish. That may be so, but I prefer to make my mixes at home, at leisure, with facilities for washing and rinsing my hands and receptacles thoroughly. There, I am also able to measure and record various ingredients and experiment a little with additives. For the actual mixing it is far better to use a round shallow bowl rather than a deep container. It is easier then to ensure that none is missed by being 'hidden' in corners. The liquid, usually water, should be introduced a little at a time, working the mix until a light, fluffy, crumbly mix is achieved. Make sure all the tap water is run until the chlorioration has dissipated by leaving it to stand.

Liquid flavour additives should be mixed with the water before addition to the crumb and any powdered additive or colouring agent thoroughly dispersed in the crumb before use. Keep your hands and any receptacles clean and well rinsed, just in case and contamination is accidentally introduced. By contamination, I mean body chemicals we all exude through the skin, for instance. Work the mix until almost reaching the point where the mix can be formed into small balls and held in the palm of the hand without it breaking it up too easily. Take it to the water in that state, adding the final touch with a plant spray gun or similar. Good judgement and experience are required to get it just right, I admit, but when you do the effort pays dividends.

Incidentally, a little dry rusk will enliven a groundbait. Poke a hole in a ball with your finger and put in a little dry rusk. Seal off the hole and, once in the water, the rusk absorbs moisture so quickly it will force the ball apart. Test it at home and watch your 'time-bomb' mix particles moving attractively. Any good butcher can supply you with rusk quite cheaply. Please remember that groundbait badly made up so that it does not break down easily and is, in effect, a modgy, lumpy mass, will feed the fish and will not attract them. However, practice will make a fast or slow sinking cloud of really attractive bait, among which your hook bait will be unique.

Your enticing groundbait may well attract fish, but hungry shoals may well disperse again if they find nothing to hold them there. A little feed added to the mix should do the trick. Remember, such feed should, if possible, be of slightly inferior quality to the hookbait. Nor should the amount be overdone. A few tempting scraps are all that is needed if the fish are not, again, to be quickly satisfied and lose interest. Larger, more cagey specimens may be waiting in the wings. They could be sparked off by the feeding of eager lesser brethren, often being less cautious and first on the scene. The feeding, on the little and often routine, should aim to prolong activity in the swim as long as possible. Even on those rare occasions when you have a good head of voraciously feeding fish which seem to belie over feeding - take care! *What has been introduced to the swim cannot be removed.* There are few golden rules in angling, as I've already said, but there is one; *Always make sure your groundbait, feed and hookbait are in the same place at the same time!*

Feeding Aids

The popular catapult and swimfeeder help us to follow that golden rule. The swimfeeder neatly solves the problem of acting as leger or paternoster weight while carrying groundbait, feed and hookbait area every time. All the angler needs to do is to be consistent in his casting technique. A whole new style of fishing has evolved round the feeder with specialist tackle and rods, usually with swing, spring and quiver-tip indicators. On the other hand, the catapult demands its own skill in use, especially when the wind is evident, aiming and grouping groundbait often being difficult. When wind or the limit of catapult range makes it impossible, especially with feed such as maggot, the feeder float can be used as an alternative. It is a hollow-bodied waggler type of float which allows a trickle of maggots to fall in close to the hookbait. You don't see it used much, perhaps anglers preferring to turn to the swimfeeder in such circumstances. Take care when it is used, however, for fish have a marked tendency to be drawn towards the surface by the trickle of maggots.

Talk of swimfeeders reminds me of a pet dislike. Most feeders, if they have cap ends at all, have those which are a push-fit. Some have a screw fit which I find cross-thread very easily. They can be the very devil, when fingers are cold and wet, to undo! Or is it me? A dodge to reduce the rate at which live feed escapes from a feeder is to partially block off some of the holes with adhesive tape.

Catapults

Catapults are sold with a wide variety of strength and a good variety of pouches, usually perforated, which allows for the firing of baits ranging from rock hard boilies to the caster. The perforated cups are usually for caster and maggot, as well as seed baits such as hemp, tares, chick peas and pulses, etc. A hard cup, or leather strip, is usually meant for boilies, but until a skill or knack is acquired in their use, the unwary is likely to suffer from rapped knuckles. It is, however, an aid towards acquiring the skill!

The average pleasure angler may well get away with using two catapults; one for maggots and one for groundbait, say, but the all-round angler, equipped for every eventuality, might well find a use for four of different strength and design, from a lightweight maggot 'pult' to a heavy boilie firer. I have four plus a throwing stick.

Throwing Sticks

The throwing stick, in the right hands, is a quick and accurate means of putting out feed. Despite this, they do not seem to be as popular as the catapult. Although they can be bought, most anglers would be capable of making their own cheaply enough. A tube of metal or plastic about two feet long and about two inches in diameter, plugged to a depth of three inches at one end to hold the feed, and if you prefer it, a handgrip at the other, which is ideal for throwing maggots, caster and the like. For boilies a deeper cup needs to be formed in a tube of slightly bigger diameter than the largest tube of slightly bigger diameter than the largest boilie used. It should be plugged ten or twelve inches from one end and then the boilies can be ejected at high velocity, so much so, it is possible to split them under such force. For long distance baiting, they are ideal.

Baitdroppers

Gardner market one under the name of Bait Rocket. This type can also be home-made. It is a cone or cup of plastic or similar, well perforated to reduce air resistance and to allow it to empty and be easily retrieved, for it is cast out by rod. The bottom of the cylinder is very buoyant that means it discharges its contents of nuts, seeds or even boilies wherever it lands on the water. Having said that, it is cast to the required spot, left on slack line while it empties, and then wound in. Normally, the bottom is filled with polystyrene. It is mainly used to prebait a swim at distance rather than while fishing. Repeated casts quickly lay down a carpet of feed. It is often called a 'spod'. The second baitdropper is a metal or plastic device that opens when it hits the bottom, laying maggots, casters, etc. It is too complicated for anglers to make, but is fairly well distributed throughout tackle shops.

Rafts and Boats

Small rafts have been used to put out feed but they are sow and limited by wind and drift. Slicker by far are the radio-controlled boats with ingenious release devices. Undeniably they reach parts of the water others do not or cannot reach, wherein perhaps, lies the reason for their dislike by other anglers.

PVA

Finally, there is a range of PVA products to aid with rig assembly and putting out loose feed. There is PVA string, bags, tapes and sleeves. PVA dissolves in cold water so that feed, to be put out in bags, for instance, has to be dry, or you will soon find a bag bursts too soon, scattering the bait anywhere. Sod's law states that it will rain whenever I want to use PVA! PVA string or thread is, I suspect, the most used form. As a means of end-rig assembly and loose feed stringer rigs, PVA string comes into its own. Its unique property of dissolving, yet its strength when dry, makes its use as a temporary assembly first class and its 'carrier' property ideal for getting loose feed and hookbait in the same place. The tape is used for securely mounting heavy fish bait in pike tackle while the sleeve form is good for mounting end-rigs and free feed in the same package. Bear in mind though, even a small bag of bait is hardly aerodynamic.

Learning a Swim

Every swim in the land is different in some ways from all the others. Seemingly identical swims may change their depths by the hour. In fact, it is a good idea to make a habit in such places by sticking a twig or something in the very edge of the water nearby to note the registration of change of depth during a session. Critical setting of float depth can be important, for instance, it is no exaggeration to say that a float just tripping a river bed at the start of a session can, within a short space of time, become a shot-dragger when water is running off or a mid-water rig when the river is rising. Still water does not alter in depth so rapidly but the accurate plumbing of a swim is still a necessity. The more you know about the topography of a water, running or still, the better. The best way to learn this is by a boat, if one is available and permission given to use it. Apart from a plumbline, a very long pole is an advantage, as is a small rake.

This work of surveying the water is best carried out when there is no-one else on the water, so that you do not interfere with the pleasures of others. Take detailed notes and draw up a map of the whole water, noting not only various depths, but the nature of the bottom, its weed types and the extent of their growth in terms of height and weed width. Note ledges, shelves, bars, 'islands' that barely reach the surface, gullies, etc, and try and deduce with your long pole the nature of each area, be it hard, gravel or soft silt. Knowing the depth of mud and soft silt can be useful, as is the various weed growths. You don't have to be a botanist, simply try and determine whether the weed grows to the surface or midwater, or both! Then you are not casting out blindly, hoping your bait is lying attractively in sight, when it could be hidden in dense weed, caught up in midwater weed, or even have sunk out of sight into soft silt. In particular, look for exposed areas within or beyond areas of weed, and if you have to fish into weed, know which species you are likely to encounter.

Feeding a Swim

The pleasure angler away from familiar waters, on holiday for example, may be faced with a swim about which he knows nothing and will have to rely on local information to give him some idea of its nature. A quick check with a plumb-line will verify such meagre information as is available, giving a rough idea of its depth. Any information is better than none. On an unknown swim, if I was so placed, for the first half-hour or so I would not feed at all, giving myself time to get comfortable, sort out unforeseen problems and get from any fish present; the places in the swim from which bites may come, what sort of fish there are and how many are responding to various hookbaits. In pleasure angling there is no panic, no need to rush!

A 16lb mirror carp.

Tench caught on sweetcorn.

Mitten Bridge, River Ribble.

You need a good pair of forceps
for this job.

A female of the species!

6½lb bream.

A 15lb 12oz mirror carp which was taken on a peanut twice the same day!

Another carp succumbs. Note the scales, bait and forceps.

A 15½lb mirror carp.

Various tackle.

A favourite carp swim.

A 17½lb carp.

An 18lb common carp.

A small one. Better than nothing!

Lady prepares to fish.

A tench. It pleases me!

Even a blank at that stage will teach you something, even if it is only features of the swim about which you know nothing.

Assuming one or two bites are forthcoming in the first half-hour, it may be time to introduce a little feed - and I stress *little*. If there is a positive response to this, for goodness sake don't go mad and throw out great dollops all in one go. It is far better to introduce feed little and often rather than a lot at long intervals. Even half a dozen maggots every cast, or every other cast; maybe even every third cast, will cause fish to seek out food in the area from time to time. Once the bites are coming frequently in a steady pattern, the amount of feed you put in and its frequency of introduction is a matter of experience and intuition as much as anything else. If the swim is in a river they will be drawn upstream by this trickle of food to find the source.

When fishing with a float, most anglers cast out the float tackle first, and then follow it with groundbait or loose feed. Look at it logically. While the float is settling and the hookbait sinking, perhaps slowly, fish may be biting on the drop. Take your eyes off it and turn your attention to obtaining maggots or groundbait to put out, could mean missed bites. If you are using a catapult, the rod may not even be in your hands! So, for my money, putting out feed and following it with the float makes sense.

In still water, by all means put feed out after the cast when legering or using a paternoster without a swimfeeder. For example, if you are allowing a leger to roll round in to a crease in the water - a line where the faster flow meets a slower one - trickling feed down to the crease to where the hook bait rests also makes sense.

Unlike stillwaters, on rivers it can be assumed that most of the fish are pointing upstream most of the time and angling pressure is less likely than on stillwaters. However, keep your sudden movements to a minimum. Sudden jerky moves can empty a swim in seconds, especially with chub being as timorous as they are, and barbel and dace being as skittery as they are. Having said that, chub and barbel bites are often deliberate and quite vicious, the rod top bending round, never mind the quiver tip! The ideal of course, is to have fish position in such a way it is possible to take them one at a time from the edge of a shoal. In that way you can cause the least disturbance on casting and on the playing of hooked fish. It's easy enough in stillwater but can prove difficult on rivers, even though the fish are pointing the same way. Only time and experience can do this for you; it cannot be taught from a book. To even begin, one's casting and bait introduction needs to be accurate and only practice can achieve that.

Keepnets

One other point with which almost no-one else will agree with me. If it is possible to return fish well away from your swim without too much inconvenience, do so! Not everyone agrees that fish can communicate in some way, but the fact remains that they do discharge a chemical from their bodies when in danger or under stress which other fish undoubtedly detect. Have you ever thought how much stress and fear fish undergo whilst in a keepnet and how much of that stress is known to others? It's a thought!

Prebaiting

Prebaiting is the introduction of feed into a swim before actually fishing that swim. It can take place days, hours or even minutes before, the aim being to draw fish to the swim before you start, or induce them or condition them, not only to enter the swim in expectation of finding food, but to condition them into accepting a particular food.

Used extensively in the search for carp, it is a method that can be usefully employed in the case of other species which have a predictable behaviour pattern such as tench, bream or barbel. In still waters prebaiting can be carried out on an extensive scale, several days before fishing, even in extreme cases for two or three weeks, particularly if there are but a few head of fish in the water. It may start off with the bait being spread over a wide variety of swims, the whole water in some cases, or in a few swims known to be visited by the fish. The bait is introduced until it is certain they are being eaten. Gradually the area being covered is reduced to one or two swims receiving regular attention over time. Gradually the area being covered is reduced to one or two swims receiving regular attention over time. When bait is being taken from these swims on a regular basis, the areas covered are reduced until only feed can be found in that spot. High vantage point and a pair of polaroid glasses may be needed to actually see the fish feeding, even in clear water, but if the fish are interested in the feed, you will have trained them to eat the bait where and when you want them to. All that remains is for the hookbait to be introduced! Of course, the time you do so must coincide with the prebaiting time to increase your chances. There are snags, of course. Someone else may have deduced what you are up to and followed your actions secretly, reaping rewards from your time and effort expended.

Other less hazardous prebaiting is simply to put out bait immediately before fishing, already having ascertained what they will hopefully be feeding on. Prebaiting a river swim may seem a waste of time, other than prebaiting on the day of fishing, but it is as well, if you can, to bait up two or three times during the day until you find action. Barbel are often drawn in swims by baiting up with hemp and moving from one to the other swims.

Additives

There are innumerable additives of both liquid and powdered forms now available, as well as countless flavours and essential oils with which to attract fish. Many of the latter types are now being incorporated into hookbaits as well as into groundbait mixes, hoping their addition has the edge over conventional mixes. There are also plenty of natural flavours that can be used when blended with paste baits; soup powders, custard powders, sausage, cheese and sweetcorn juice are but a few of them. To colour bait or groundbait, powdered colouring agents can be used successfully. Most people seem to agree that powdered colours at the end of the spectrum are the best, such as orange, yellow or brown. Whether you choose a dark colour on a light bed, or a light colour on a dark bed is up to you. As far as I know, there is no positive proof that it makes any difference. When any kind of additive is used it is always difficult to prove catches were made because of them. On the whole, it depends on how much confidence you place on their use.

Incidentally, to give maggots a distinctive flavour it needs no more than three or four drops of concentrated flavour on a tuft of cotton wool. The clean maggot receptacle is then wiped with the cotton-wool with the impregnated flavour. The maggots are put in along with the tuft of wool and then left overnight. 'Carp Fever', by Kevin Maddocks, (Beekay Publishers) gives much information on such matters.

Five

BAIT PRESENTATION

The manner in which bait is presented is often more important than the choice of bait itself. I have watched free offerings eaten up rapidly by small roach shoals, the fish in competition with each other, while at the other end of the spectrum I've seen large carp in small groups of two or three fish, as well as a single fish, clean up an area meticulously of every loose offering. Many times in all those cases one single bait remained untouched - the one with the hook in it! There is no reason to doubt that all species behave in the same way at times, studiously ignoring hook bait, no matter how tempting it may be. Perhaps it is only in the heat of the moment, when hunger overrides caution, or when they are so preoccupied we manage to catch them at all!

I've done a fair whack of carp fishing, read a good deal about them and have heard of the so-called superior intelligence they are said to possess. It sometimes seems to me they are afforded a degree of reasoning and acumen that surpasses the human thinking process, if you take notice of some people. No fish is that intelligent any more than any other kind of creature. Carp can be caught...no, they can't! They can be conditioned into certain responses, and if that conditioning is reinforced, they remember it. Hence my discourse in chapter two on minimising the trauma they endure on capture.

On closed waters of all sorts, repeated capture must condition fish of all kinds to be vary wary of going for food which does not behave in a natural manner, or in a way which does not spark off a conditioned reflex. I believe that to be the case, to a greater or lesser degree, with every species, not just carp. There's little doubt that carp do have the largest brains of our freshwater fish and little doubt they are the easiest to condition one way or another, although other fish seem to exhibit certain aspects of carp's behaviour. For instance, the tench is notoriously easy to catch early in the season, yet they quickly become conditioned into being wary of hookbaits as the season progresses. As this happens quite quickly, there is every reason to suppose they forget quite quickly too! Note, too, how fish in tanks and ponds respond to regular feeding. They actually assemble in the same area each time. No doubt they would soon become circumspect if one felt a hook now and again! I recall watching carp in Holland - in a public park. With a complete ban on fishing, huge carp lifted themselves out of the water to take bread from the fingers of excited children!

Why is the commercial maggot so popular with fish? It's not particularly nutritious but fish are attracted to them because they are harmless. Billions thrown into the water annually cause them no problem. Excessive angling pressure soon conditions them to be wary of those that fall into their fishy mouths, into their world, on the end of a line, no matter how fine it may be.

Below, Figs.8-10. Methods of Mounting Baits. Left to right: Breadcrust, Hemp and Tares.

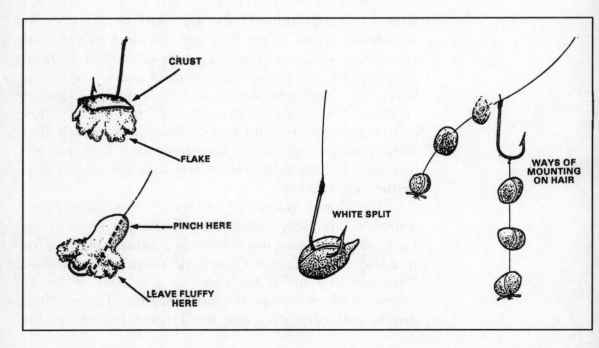

CRUST

FLAKE

PINCH HERE

LEAVE FLUFFY HERE

WHITE SPLIT

WAYS OF MOUNTING ON HAIR

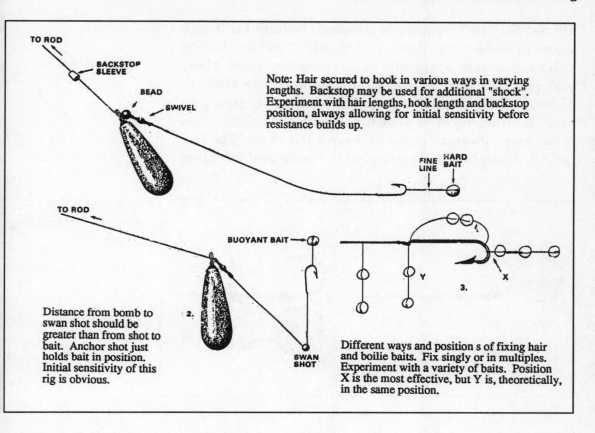

Note: Hair secured to hook in various ways in varying lengths. Backstop may be used for additional "shock". Experiment with hair lengths, hook length and backstop position, always allowing for initial sensitivity before resistance builds up.

Distance from bomb to swan shot should be greater than from shot to bait. Anchor shot just holds bait in position. Initial sensitivity of this rig is obvious.

Different ways and position s of fixing hair and boilie baits. Fix singly or in multiples. Experiment with a variety of baits. Position X is the most effective, but Y is, theoretically, in the same position.

Above: Fig.11. Methods of mounting boilie baits

All the foregoing is leading up to putting across an understanding of the waters you fish and the importance of presenting bait in as natural a manner as possible. Most of angling's literature has put up the notion that unless you behave like a 'great white hunter' at all times, tackling up away from the swim, wearing subdued colours, etc. then you will be wasting your time. If you know of a 'wild' water, rarely disturbed by man, and in that category I include rivers, unless you keep out of sight, tread warily and keep quiet, you will not catch a thing. To be so intent on keeping quiet and unseen is a joke on may waters. The garishly dressed fisherfolk humping their tackle along the bank do not conform to the writer's idea nowadays; but any water that does not have to endure angling pressure, requires from you every skill you may develop in your search for fish.

The increased travel opportunities, urban expansion and an increase in angling pressures have, in my opinion, altered the need for general advice. It is doubtful if such views as those of the 'great white hunter' have any lasting values, except in a minority of cases and on rivers. Many waters are adjacent to roads, railways and even airports. Many holiday venues the angler seeks are camping or caravan sites, most of which are subject to continuous noise and vibration virtually round the clock. The fish quickly learn that a great deal of the noise and vibration

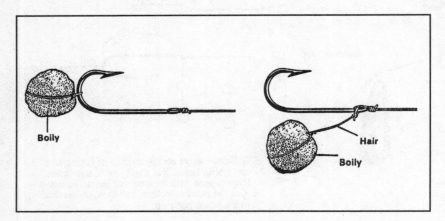

Left: Figs.12-13. Methods of Mounting Boilies.

causes them no harm at all yet they accept that there remains an angling pressure they respond to. It makes an enormous difference to their lives, differing through twenty-four hours and reaching a peak during weekends and holiday periods.

When angling is at its lowest ebb, night or day, that is the time to adopt the 'great white hunter' techniques - or when fishing in a river or any 'wild' water. So my general advice is learn what affects a water and react accordingly. When you do so, don't forget noise and vibration travels a long way under water and that fish are not really intelligent at all, but are far more sensitive than we are with our crude senses. When it is necessary, be prepared to act like primitive man, as if satiating hunger depends on spearing or catching a fish. Be like the heron, slow moving, inconspicuous and actually attuned to the job in hand. Keep as still as you are able until you are ready to strike. Keep tackle still and avoid sudden, jerky movements, which are more likely to catch the eye of the fish and scare it half to death! After all, it's a puerile exercise to fish where there are none left!

Natural Bait Behaviour

It's doubtful if a bait can ever be presented in a truly natural way as long as it is attached to a line, no matter how fine the line may be. The ideal should be aimed at, nevertheless, on hard fished hungry waters. The game fisher may take great pains over his fly-tying methods but he will try harder to make it behave as though it were real. His task is made easier by the fact that game river fish are usually caught only once! The upshot of closed game waters has altered that fact, however. The coarse angler faces an equally daunting task in some ways, made more so by the fact that the fish may be ultra shy, having suffered the trauma of capture several times, hence my discussion on how to minimise their traumatic experience.

Inducing Bites

In running water, one way to induce natural movement is to allow the bait to rise and fall temptingly and briefly as

Right: Fig.14. Method for side-hooking boilie.

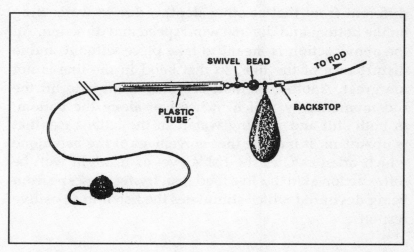

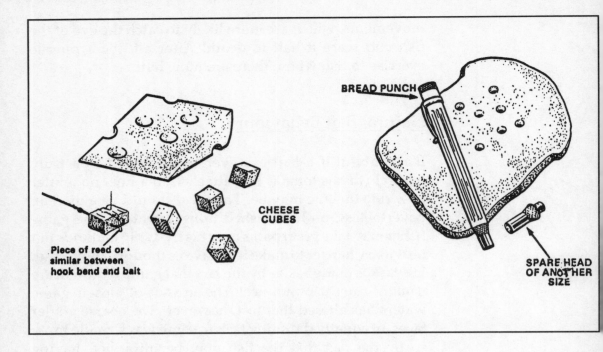

it is trotted through the swim. The Stick, Balsa and the Pacemaker floats are ideal for this, although no float should be held back too hard, causing it to lift itself in the water, but just long enough to allow the bait to rise gently and fall back. The Stick, in particular, has a tendency to rise too high when used by heavy handed anglers. The Avon float is also a good trotter, the aim being with all these floats to allow the bait to move along with the flow, which often has a surface speed different from that at other depths, due to water drag on the bottom and diverse wind speed and direction. All the above action is meant to take place without undue disturbance of the line, so that bend in the line is not too great. Another method of inducement is to lift the rod momentarily which inches bait along the bottom, in both still and moving water. In the latter case, that is upstream. It may be the movement of the bait alone which often catches the fish's eye, or it might well be reflex action akin to a live food item trying to escape from being devoured which stimulates the fish into a positive response.

Above: Figs.15-16. Bait. (left), Cheese and (right) Punched bread.

Sinking Bait

Many bites come 'on the drop', that is, before the bait has reached the limit of its fall. If you count to yourself how long it takes the float to arrive at its final stance, and then strike at the first sign of an unusual fall, you'll hit them! If you're fishing in deep water you may wish to shorten your depth. If the fish are small you may wish to increase your depth perhaps using a different rig. The choice is yours.

Legering

Below: Figs17-20. More methods of mounting bait. Left to right: (top) smear of soft paste, (bottom) hard floaters, pastes and potato.

The difficulty in legering lies in the use of the line that is used to take fish according to their size; and, of course, the nature of the bottom. This had caused many of the problems connected with carp fishing because carp are known to become rather edgy about seeing line, especially when extra width of line is used with a short leader. They are known to detour an area showing evidence of line. Some carp anglers have resorted to using an extra bomb on the line. Once the end rig is in position a second bomb is clipped to the line before the rod is placed in its nest. This set-up is best used over short distances and flat bottom.

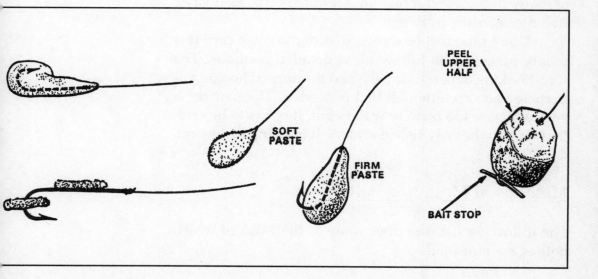

SOFT PASTE

FIRM PASTE

PEEL UPPER HALF

BAIT STOP

Carp are sought using a vast array of end-rigs designed to take surf feeding fish and bottom feeding fish. The baits are mounted as illustrated below ranging from soft seeds to soft baits and to boilies. The battle for good hooklengths and hair rigs continues unabated to the point where the carp have returned to straightforward baits and not the hair rig. I mention the hook length in this context because a braided line can become waterlogged by long immersion, though relatively supple. Dacron is as good as any. Many alternatives have been tried such as dental

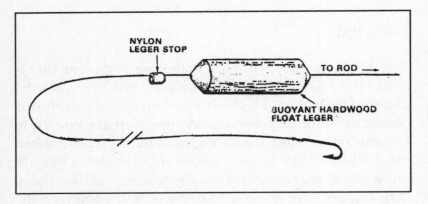

NYLON
LEGER STOP

TO ROD →

BUOYANT HARDWOOD
FLOAT LEGER

Left: Fig.21. Floater control. This "fleger" can be made of any buoyant material to give added casting range to floater baits. It also adds a little control to surface fishing when wind or drift allows. Watch the bait not the "fleger". Some woods are buoyant enough to allow the addition of a lead strip for extra range.

floss for the hair. The latest innovation has been the multi-strand type of line, supremely supple and immensely strong for its diameter. It seems to have solved the problems of many in the short term. No doubt the carp, as always, will discover the problem.

Don't imagine, however, in order to catch carp it is vitally necessary to follow these detailed methods. The side-hooking of the paste baits and the normal hooking of particle baits are often all that is needed. The hair rig is very effective too on may waters but, it needs to be said, that on very heavily fished waters, it is losing its impact.

Methods of Mounting Baits

The following list describes some of the ways in which boilies are mounted:

In Fig.11.2 fix the boilie - a buoyant boilie at the bend of the hook and add just enough weight, marked swan shot, to very, very slowly sink the hook and bait. Test it in shallow margin. Get it right and it's a killer! The boilie diameter should be slightly smaller than the hook! The methods of mounting in Figs. 12 and 13 are very effective. Fig.14 is used for side-hooking boilie.

Cheese may not require any kind of retention, especially in winter when it is likely to be hard due to cold weather, but other baits such as bacon grill, Luncheon Meat, Spam, etc., may require either a piece of grass or reed slid between the bait and the hookbend to keep the bait in situ while being cast. See Fig.15.

Bread is a versatile bait and can be used on quite small hooks with the help of a bread punch. The punch nozzle has a slit in the side into which the hook point is placed to withdraw the bread, ready for use. See Fig.16.

The diagrams shown are largely self-explanatory. The hemp seed, like all seeds, should be soaked and cooked until they begin to open up and reveal their white inner. With tiny hooks, gently open the seed case and insert the hook almost completely, so that the hook point sticks out of the split. Then gently close the split on the hook. Multi-particle hairs shown with tares are ideal for mini-boilies. An alternative is to smear the hook shank with superglue and immerse the hook in seed until it is covered. The hard floaters, dog and cat biscuits, may also be superglued in position.

The floater control, shown in Fig.21, is used in conjunction with all types of floater when extra range is required.

FISH IDENTIFICATION

Overleaf are shown the main physical features of fish which are used to identify various species, often by comparison of colour, size, shape and position in relation to those similar features in other species. Expert dissection

The Pleasures of Coarse Fishing

is often required to establish species by study of internal organs, notably the pharangeal teeth.

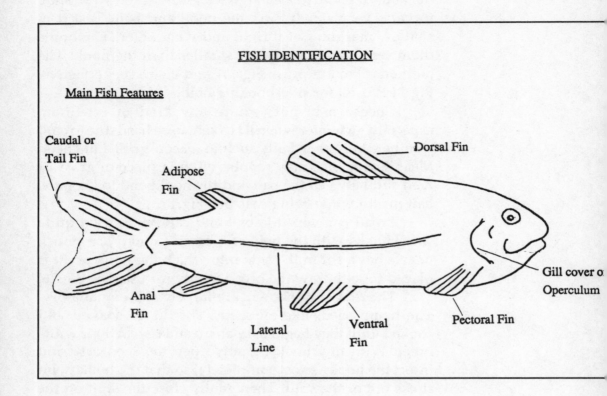

FISH IDENTIFICATION

Main Fish Features

Caudal or Tail Fin

Adipose Fin

Dorsal Fin

Anal Fin

Lateral Line

Ventral Fin

Pectoral Fin

Gill cover o Operculum

Six

FLOAT FISHING TECHNIQUES

I have to say, I have no experience of the pole and little of match fishing, preferring to indolently, some would say lazily, enjoy myself pleasure angling with a float in the way I do without that what would be to me a rather alien and remote method of catching fish. I'm well aware of the thousands of anglers who devote themselves to the not inconsiderable skills associated with those two aspects of angling. Neither, I'm afraid, appeal to me nor am I unduly concerned with the finer points of float fishing and myriad shotting patterns, the few I use being successful in my terms. To those who wish to delve deeper into such matters, I would suggest they consult the comprehensive study on the subject in *The Complete Book of Float Fishing*, by Allen Haines, published by David and Charles. My comments are confined to the aspects of float fishing I have found useful, including general hints, tips and advice I feel would be useful to others.

Basic Shotting Patterns for Waggler and Joggler

Everyone knows what a waggler is. It's a float attached to a line at the bottom end only. More correctly, it is the style of fishing with the float so fixed. No-one knows what a joggler is - except me! It's my way of describing a float attached to the line at both ends. More properly it's a style of fishing with a float so fixed.

Fig.22 shows the basic three shotting patterns on which all the others are based. Although only wagglers

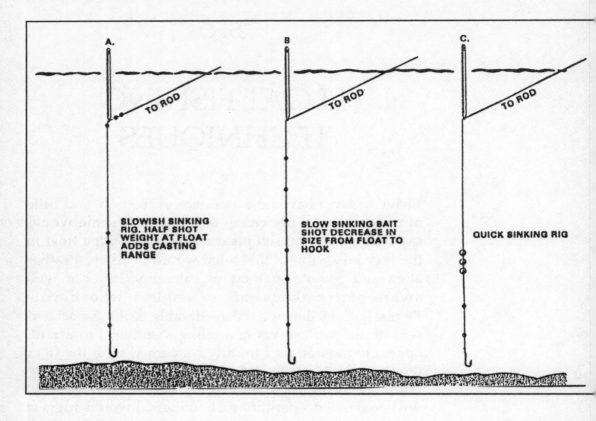

Above: Fig.22. The three basic shotting patterns.

are shown, it does include jogglers. Fig.22 (A) is usually applied to the waggler with half to two thirds of the shotting weight used as a locking shot to set the float at the depth required. The remainder of the shot must be set between the mid-mark between float and hook, which includes the indicator shot. A waggler so shotted acts in a way similar to a zoomer, the shot at the float base aiding its casting further. The rest of the shot, if set as advised avoids a tendency to tangle, and gives a rather slowish sinking bait. The shot pattern (B) shows the evenly spaced shotting most often used with joggler floats such as the Stick or Avon types. It offers a slow sinking bait that induces many bites 'on the drop' as well as offering a degree of control when wanting to allow a bait to rise temporarily in the water by checking the float's progress briefly in running water. Fig.22 (C) demonstrates the patterns used to get the bait down quickly with the shot weight grouped tightly below the mid-mark twixt float and hook with the hope of larger brethren. It is also used for plummeting bait down through weed, or to act as a kind of stabiliser on the windbeater rig, to name but three of its uses.

Fig.23 shows some of the many types of floats on the market while Fig.24 shows correct and incorrect setting of a Ducker float or any other waggler style. Fig.24 (A) is a rig with a standard shot setting for mid-water fishing at a chosen depth. Fig.24 (B) shows the change in pattern to a loaded or weighted waggler, but as far as sensitivity goes it is incorrectly set, being well over the depth. In fact, if you wish to 'lay on' and many fish are caught that way, the rig (A) is better. The waggler rig at (C) has the most sensitivity, only the baited hook actually resting lightly on the bottom. The simple lift-bite rig using a quill, anchored by one shot is shown in Fig.25. A very effective one rig it is, too! If conditions call for the use of a heavier float, wind or drift

Right: Fig.23. Some of the many types of float available.

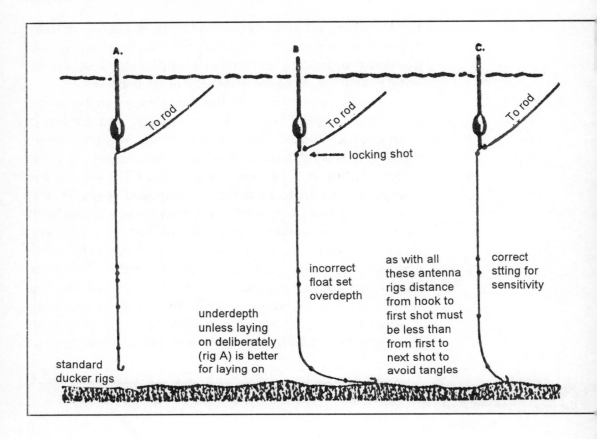

Above: Fig.24. Correct and incorrect settings of a Ducker float.

being a problem, for example, or you may want to cast farther than the one-shot quill will allow, the Windbeater rig is a good choice. It is designed for stability and it can be used as a slider float. It is easily visible, the long antenna with its intermittent coloration and its sight-bulb at the tip being advantageous towards that end. To use it at its best, its most sensitive, however, calls for a little care in the addition of the shot. The grouped bulk of the shot, while cocking the float and perhaps settling in down the water, should NOT sink it. Only the addition of the lift shot should do that, for me the slower the better. If it sinks slowly it will rise slowly when the bait is lifted by a fish. This gives plenty of time for the angler to react, strike and set the hook. A lively method of fishing. I've caught many a tench and carp on this rig.

Fishing Waggler Style

The method I use for waggler float fishing is by the means of a push-fit adaptor, the use of which allows a quick change of float without breaking down the whole rig to do so. The locking-shot, when used, is placed either side of the Silicon adaptor usually with a back-up locking-shot to prevent float slippage during repeated casting.

The float behaves best in the cast when all the shot are set closer to the hook than the float as suggested in Fig.24, casting farther without repeated tangles, but you have to make certain the indicator shot is placed at LESS distance from the hook than from the next shot up the line!

Another advantage of the waggler is that it allows the line to be submerged between the float and rod tip to minimise the effect of wind or drift. The way to do this and retain the bait in the chosen position is to overcast slightly and as soon as the rig hits the water sink the rod top and give two or three quick turns of the reel, quickly sinking the line and pulling the rig back into position. With a bit of practice this little routine becomes almost automatic and inevitably more accurate in execution. The waggler also comes into its own on the river in a downstream wind or more than a rod length out from the fishing position taking over from the jogglers that become virtually useless in those cases being very difficult to control properly if not impossible.

Fig.23 shows a handful of floats which can be used waggler style showing size including buoyancy distribution and antenna length and diameter which are available. There are literally hundreds on the market including Duckers, Windbeaters, Peacocks and the large seemingly oversized Cocktail float; floats, in fact, for every conceivable eventuality.

Floats for a set of particular circumstances are a good buy and it has to be said that floats have improved in manufacture over the years. Drennan and Middy floats are among the best of them.

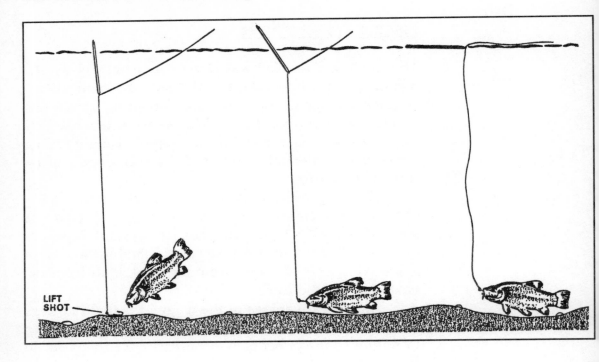

Above: Fig.25. A simple lift-bite rig using a quill, anchored by one shot.

Fishing Joggler Style

The joggler, you may recall, is my way of describing a float attached to the line at top and bottom; double rubbered, as they say.

Their main use is for trotting a swim when river fishing - although I do remember successful boyish jaunts when we fished for, and caught, almost every species you care to mention including good bronze bream using a cork-bodied Avon type float in both river and stillwater fishing.

Anyhow, the choice now is to select a joggler best suited for the degree and speed of turbulence of the river, the idea being to emulate a free offering being moved along by the current, whether it be slow and placid or fast and turbulent, whether it be deep or shallow. The drawbacks encountered in joggler use are that they cannot be controlled at much more than a rod length out they are next to unless in a downstream wind. In those circumstances, as it has already been said, the waggler takes over.

Controlling a joggler trot is best done from directly behind its run, from upstream of it, checking the float's progress gently, even to the point of allowing the bait to swing forward and rise in the current as though lifted temporarily by it. It is often enough to cause a fish to bite or at least draw the fish's attention to the bait. Bear in mind the float is always more likely to be in advance of the bait when trotting, the flow at the surface being faster than the flow at the bottom, unless the wind dictates otherwise.

In certain conditions a small trotter will look after itself, negotiating quite turbulent water on its own, while the larger versions respond to line control better and retain greater stability during line manipulation.

Shot Dragging Technique

Below: Fig.26. The Windbeater or Driftbeater float.

As shown in Fig.26 this technique can be effective for chub, barbel and the occasional good roach in deepish swims of moderate flow. The evenly spaced shotting

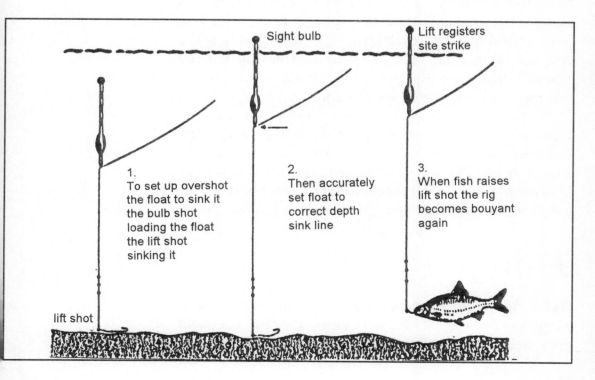

Sight bulb

Lift registers
site strike

1.
To set up overshot
the float to sink it
the bulb shot
loading the float
the lift shot
sinking it

2.
Then accurately
set float to
correct depth
sink line

3.
When fish raises
lift shot the rig
becomes bouyant
again

lift shot

pattern and a greased line are a good help. Easing the slightly bellied line along at the desired speed, not allowing too much of a belly lest striking problems arise. When using a waggler for shot dragging the pattern in Fig.24(C) is more generally used, the line being sunk between float and rod tip.

Zoomer Fishing

There are several ways to make a simple zoomer, the quickest of all being the addition of a shot near the base, as in Fig.28.

The zoomer float is sensitive and will cast an impressive distance. Its purpose is to cast close to objects in the water in which other rigs may become entangled, whereas the zoomer precedes the hook in flight. If you wish to fish close to weedbeds on a lake or moored boats on a canal, for instance, this is the rig to use. Accuracy of cast is essential. A good trick often used to sustain accuracy of distance on repeated casting, is to slip a broad elastic band over the reel spool, once you have found the exact distance. On subsequent casts, you should hit the spot every time! The line will be checked from leaving the spool by the elastic band, making you look good, by the way!

There's always the risk of the hook catching up on the line with this rig but it does not happen as often as you would think. The waggler shotted rig, which is similar in principle, would overcome the problem, but could be too cumbersome and heavy for surface feeding rudd.

Slider Float Usage

Slider floats are used widely in coarse fishing, both waggler and joggler types being employed. The float eyes need to be relatively small and the float itself

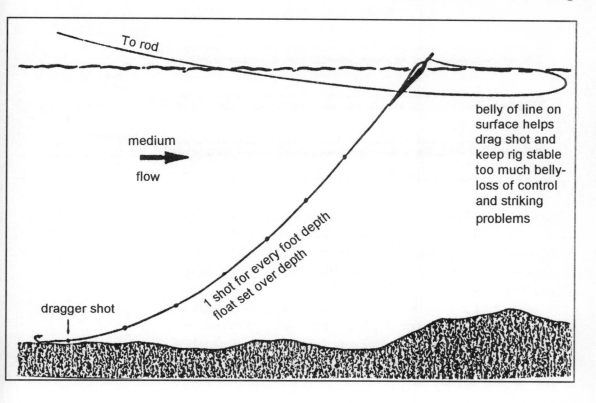

To rod

medium → flow

belly of line on surface helps drag shot and keep rig stable too much belly- loss of control and striking problems

1 shot for every foot depth float set over depth

dragger shot

Above: Fig.27. The Avon or Balsa Shot Dragger.

relatively buoyant. Usually, shotting needs to be grouped and fairly heavy, all of which assists the sliding action to take place, as shown in Fig.30.

The reasons for using the sliding float are, one, when the depth is greater than the rod length and, two, when fishing with bushes, trees and other restrictions close behind you, allowing overhead casting where it would otherwise have been impossible.

When the float hits the water, immediately allow plenty of slack line. This lets the line start running through the float eye, as shown.

Other Uses

The sliding float is not just used as a waggler, as shown in Fig.30. The joggler slider is used with the insertion of a pin high on the body of a large Balsa. Some of these sliders are used in pike fishing. Some are made of

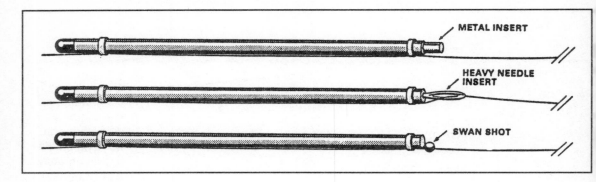

Above: Fig.28. Ways of making a simple zoomer float.

hollow plastic with a narrow tube running through them from tip to base. Such floats are used to suspend heavy baits which may be on the bottom or held in mid-water. A stopknot is used to set the depth, and the float may or may not be seen.

I am not a fanatic about pike fishing, although I would not scorn the odd pike trip, but if anyone is interested in knowing more about the use of pike floats, *The Complete Specimen Hunter,* by Tony Miles will produce many of the answers.

THE FLOAT AND THE PATERNOSTER

It seems natural to examine the float-leger techniques

Below: Fig.29. A zoomer in action.

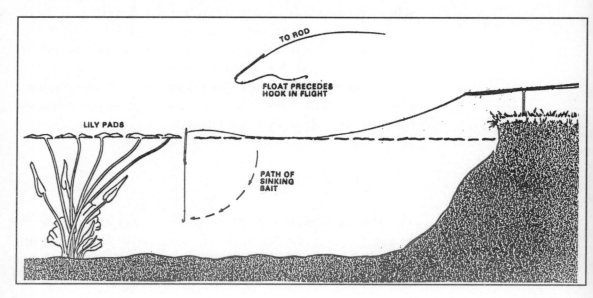

and the paternoster before moving into legering proper. It is also a good place to have a look at various leger and float stops.

Leger Stops

The commercial stops vary in size and are easily obtainable but they can be difficult to undo at times and can, if over-tightened, damage and weaken line. Used with a relatively light tackle and mounted with care, they are a reliable stop. The stop-shot suffers from the same disadvantages, being a bit fiddly as well as line damaged by an overzealous angler. I am less inclined to trust the stop-shot, especially now they are of a non-toxic alloy and are not made of lead.

On heavier tackle a swivel is a much better bet, providing a stop for the leger and a swivelled link for the hook length. A bead is invariably inserted between the leger weight and the swivel to give protection from the weight of the lead to the line knot. Even so, line can quickly become suspect from the pressure applied by heavy, long-distance casts. It is well worth inspecting such rigs at regular intervals, looking for any flattening or fraying of the line.

Float Stops

These are now commercially available. The Dam float-stop is good and is re-useable, but being me I tend to lose them, reverting as often as not, to a stop knot shown in Fig.5.

The Stopstick

A form of stop I have used for many years now, *where it can be safely applied*, is the stopstick, as I call it. It can be used as a float stop, but NOT when circumstances

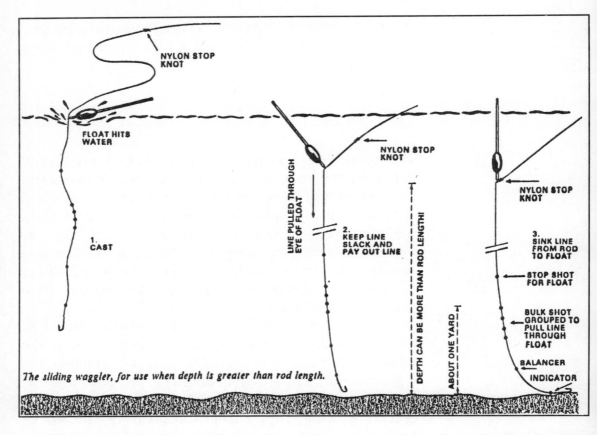

The sliding waggler, for use when depth is greater than rod length.

would bring the stopstick to the rod, preventing retrieval - nor would I use it as a stop where the swivel is essential!

Above: Fig.30. Slider float usage.

There are, however, many instances where it can be used to advantage, the line is never damaged no matter how many times it is used which is a great advantage. It never slips and is very easy to make,

All you need is about half an inch of softwood. A paired down match is fine. Cut two small pieces off a biro inner tube, and you have it! The two pieces are threaded onto the line and the matchstick is inserted in them at both ends. Once the wood is wet it swells and fits snugly in the tubing. For extra security the line can be twisted once or twice before the second tube is fitted. See Fig.31.

No line damage, no slippage, easily moved and re-useable: this little companion you'll find is a cracker!

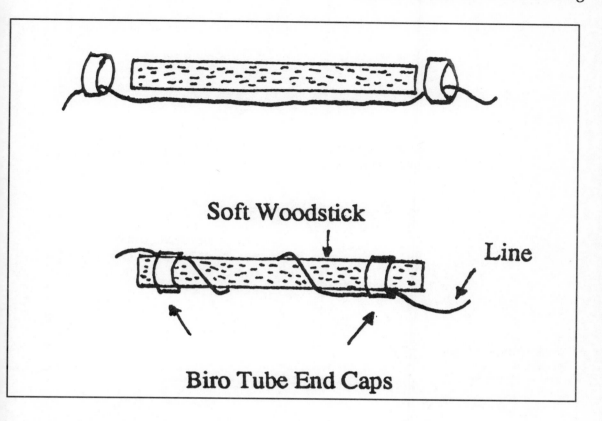

Soft Woodstick

Line

Biro Tube End Caps

Above: Fig.31. The Stopstick.

The Float Leger Method

Fishing with a float leger is a successful and very enjoyable method for the pleasure angler to use. Advocated by Len Arbery for use with a buoyant bait, or pop-up, in his book, *Catching Big Tench*, yet summarily dismissed by none other than Richard Walker in *Successful Angling* as having been superseded by more modern developments, even then, stating that the float's buoyancy acts as a resistance to biting fish, although he was not advocating pop-up baits, which does make a difference. I can only say, having used it for years to the present day, that there is truth in both versions.

So where does the pleasure angler go from there? Which of these two great anglers do you believe? Both, I would suggest, for both are right, looking at the rig from differing angles or aspects. Like every other rig, it may have disadvantages, but it still catches fish!

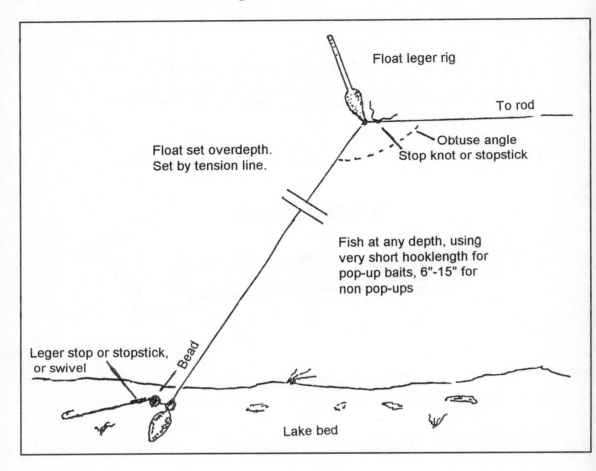

Above: Fig.32. Setting up the float leger.

I myself have used it for tench in a similar way to Arbery, using a waggler. I've caught chub on it in suitable river conditions using a joggler, the bait being cheese or bread. Decent roach have been taken on corn, perch (though not very big ones) on worm. They could have caught on other rigs, admittedly. It's successful with carp too.

The diagram above, Fig.32, shows how to set it up, the float cocked by tension between bomb and rod tip. A waggler with a long antenna is ideal. It can be used in areas too far out for the other float rigs, the only limitation being antenna visibility.

The Paternoster Principle

Advantages of the paternoster are not very obvious until you think about it.

A)   It can hold a bait at a fixed position from the bottom, irrespective of the depth of water.

B)   It overcomes drift while suspending a bait in mid-water.

Below: Fig.33. A pater-noster for deep water can be either fixed or sliding, depending on the type of presentation required.

C)   It actually anchors a bait in a fixed position, so the degree of swim disturbance is minimal.

D)   It offers an alternative form of bait presentation to either the float or the leger - a valuable asset when fish are

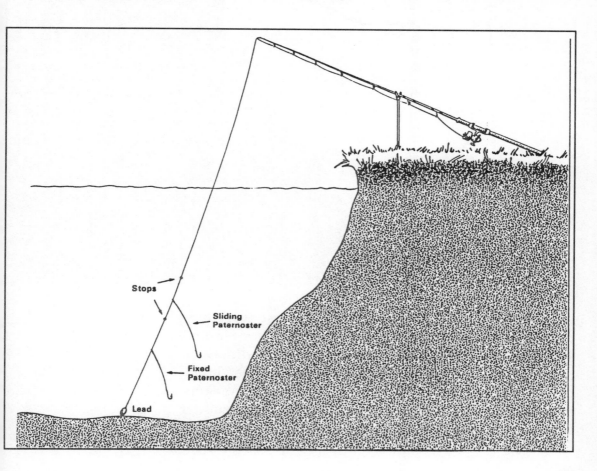

Stops

Sliding
Paternoster

Fixed
Paternoster

Lead

'educated' to the alternatives mentioned.

E)   In deep water a suspended paternoster can be used to find at what depths the fish are feeding and what bait they prefer by the use of two hooklengths on the same main line, thus obviating the need to tie up two rods to do so. Be sure two hook set-ups are allowed where you fish, however!

By using stop shots or stopsticks, one or both paternostered

Below: Fig.34. The use of a float is an alternative to keeping the rod high.

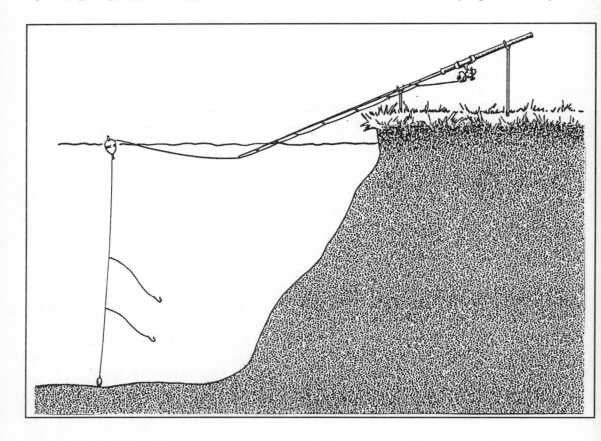

hooklengths can be used as sliders. Almost everything drawn or written about in angling literature requires some form of modification to suit local conditions or personal preference. Listing advantages, as above, should readily spell out possible solutions to local problems. Although the sea angler is well versed in paternoster usage, the coarse angler perhaps needs to be reminded

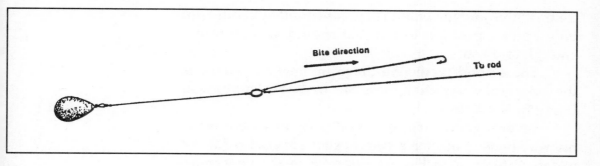

Above: Fig.35.   that the suspended paternoster is eminently suitable for fishing from a boat or the side of a very deep water with steep banks, he being more familiar with using it for bottom fishing worth swimfeeder or bomb in much shallower waters and less steep banking.

As suggested in the section on slider-floats, heavier versions are almost legendary, however, in pike fishing circles.

Bottom Fishing

Figs. 35 and 36 show how important it is to retrieve the line after the cast until you can feel the bomb link; it gives the fish little or no immediate resistance to the bite. The bait can be sucked from all directions. It also gives the most immediate indication at the rod end. If the fish panics and runs *towards* the rod, dragging the bomb with it, you will get a drop-back bite; that is, a curved quiver tip will straighten out and any kind of bobbin will fall, not rise. It is wise, then, to set your indicators in a position in which they *can* react to drop-backs! The swing-tip should be able to fall, the quiver-tip

Below: Fig.36.

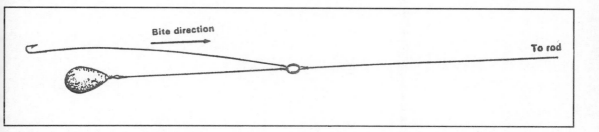

to straighten and the bobbin or grease monkey should not only be in a position to fall, but should also be heavy enough to do so!

The second factor the diagrams make obvious, is the enormous variation possible in hook length and bomb link length.

Several good carp into double figures have come my way by way of such a paternoster. This is due I think to the difference such a rig offers from the new more usual leger rigs. Tench, too, have taken on such rigs when all else failed. The carp were taken on luncheon meat, as shown below, while the tench fell for golf ball sized balls of sausage meat paste, etc, a mix of sausage meat and ground Weetabix, I recall. In the latter case, the hook was buried in the heart of the ball, while the luncheon meat was 'secured' with a blade of grass between the bait and the hook bend.

In somewhat schematic diagrams, in Figs. 35 and 36, the ring could be used as shown or the paternostered hooklength secured by a water knot. In heavier rigs a three-way swivel could be used but with lighter rigs using swimfeeder and swingtip, for instance the principle of drawing the line back until the hooklength is sensitive to bites and allows the bite to give positive indication.

Seven

A LOOK AT LEGERING

Lead Weight Variations

Many of the old leger patterns are still available, albeit of non-toxic alloys if they are less than one ounce in weight.

The barrel, coffin and bullet are the three mostly still available, all drilled centrally and a leger stop used to prevent the weight running down to the hook, thus establishing hooklength. They are crude direct legers by modern standards but still have their uses. The coffin lead will often hold the bottom in running water, while the barrel and bullets can be used to roll round slowly while searching for fish on clear, flat areas of river bed.

The Link Leger

Once a leger has a device for offsetting the main line from the weight it becomes properly a link leger. Even the Arlesey bomb falls into this category.

Below: Figs.37-38. (left), Barrel lead and coffin lead, and (right) bullet.

The simplest form of link leger you can produce yourself is to form a loop of line over the main line and fix

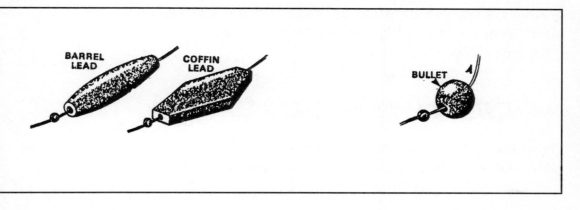

several large shots to it. This is best done by centrally placing the shot with all the splits facing the same way which is the correct method for grouping shot, even in float rigs.

It's a great little dodge for use as a sensitive light leger in both still and running water but is at its most useful in river fishing

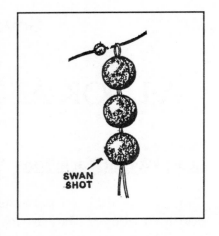

Left: Fig.39. Swan shot.

when leger weight is critical, shot being added and subtracted until it just, and only just, holds bottom. It can also be used, of course, in paternoster form by fixing it to the main line, either direct, as it is, or on a longer link.

In Silt, Soft Mud, And Over Weed

In such situations the true link leger will assist in solving the problem. In its simplest form it is but a line tied to a bomb at one end and to a leger head at the other. The main line is then threaded through the bead as opposed to the swivel-eye, as shown in Fig.42.

A piece of buoyant material such as cork, balsa wood or polystyrene can be used to keep the main line above weed, keeping it clear and free running. See Fig.40.

The reason I usually use diamond-eyed swivels on my hooklengths when used at all, is that I think they fit the grinner knot more snugly into the bead which protects the knots from damage. Still, I invariably check leger rigs quite frequently, just in case.

ELEMENTS OF A MODERN LEGER SET-UP

Fig.41 shows the main features of a typical modern leger set-up. Great changes are possible overall, particularly in

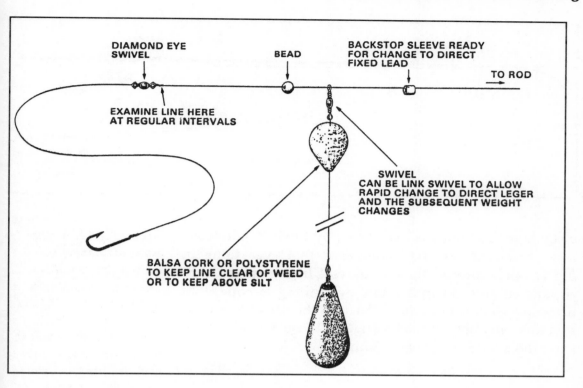

DIAMOND EYE
SWIVEL

BEAD

BACKSTOP SLEEVE READY
FOR CHANGE TO DIRECT
FIXED LEAD

TO ROD

EXAMINE LINE HERE
AT REGULAR INTERVALS

SWIVEL
CAN BE LINK SWIVEL TO ALLOW
RAPID CHANGE TO DIRECT LEGER
AND THE SUBSEQUENT WEIGHT
CHANGES

BALSA CORK OR POLYSTYRENE
TO KEEP LINE CLEAR OF WEED
OR TO KEEP ABOVE SILT

Above: Fig.40. A link leger with the added refinement of a floating ball to keep the swivel clear of weed or silt.

the end-rig presentation, points A-C and in indication methods at points E-H and at point D.

A commonly used set-up of end-rig (A-C) is shown in Fig.42. In this illustration the backstop C can be dispensed with or set at any distance behind the bomb. This results in an initial lack of resistance and as the fish takes up the bait and begins to move away it is suddenly 'jolted' by the backstop hitting the bomb, turning the bite into a full-blooded run.

Have another look at Figs. 41 and 42. Fig.42 is the end-rig of a heavy leger set-up, with the bomb weight ranging from one to two and a half ounces, for example. It's the standard rig, if you like, from which a plethora of rig variations have been developed. There are almost as many books on the subject as there are rigs. Those interested could do worse than consult a modern classic, if only for a thorough appraisal of the bait scene, parts of which are not only useful to carp anglers, but of other species, too many of the ideas and principles now being applied

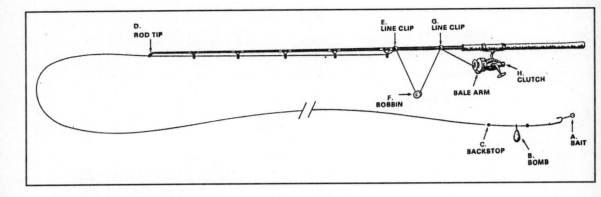

elsewhere. The book is *Carp Fever*, by Kevin Maddocks.

It should also be understood that everything in Fig.41 can be altered: the rod, the reel, line diameter, end-rig and method of indication, everything to cope with differing species of venues. Perhaps the use of line clips remains a mystery for some anglers, those not yet having tried the mysteries of carp fishing.

Above: Fig.41. A schematic diagram of the main legering features. The angler has control in two main areas: AC and DH. With the line clipped at E there will be no movement at F until it is pulled free. A clip at G allows free movement of F.

Line Clip Usage

The clip at point G, I set over, or almost over the reel spool. It helps to retain line on the spool when fishing with an open bail-arm and it sets and holds in position, the monkey climber or bobbin. If you have ever set one, you'll know why I prefer a reel to have as many backwind stops as possible!

The clip at point E is used to prevent indicator movement caused by wind or drift; two pulling at the main line, giving false bites. Nothing is more annoying, especially at night! Even so, I will attempt a cure by sinking the line before resorting to a clip at E, mainly because you get no response at all from fish activity prior to a full-blooded run!

The Swimfeeder

A whole new fishing style has arisen from the development of the swimfeeder, now available in a wide variety of designs, many on sale with their own built-in swivels and linkage systems, and with them a range of modern light-legering rods.

The bobbin, F in Fig.41, can be anything - a piece of silver paper, a lump of dough pinched onto the line or the coloured top from a washing-up liquid bottle. All of these have been superseded by modern designs, many with the facility for adding a Betalite or a similar form of night indicator. However, the bobbin, no matter what its form, is prone to movement in the wind, and although there are ways of anchoring it on a loose line fitted to the main line with a hair type of clip, so that it is not lost on the strike, despite its superior sensitivity over the latest innovations, monkey-climber and grease-monkey types are far more controllable and stable, once set. They slide up and down a metal 'ariel', the bobbin remaining on it at all times - a boon whilst fishing in the dark or in high winds! All these butt-end types can be used with or without electronic indicators such as the wheel-roller Optonic.

Below: Fig.42. A commonly used end-rig set-up.

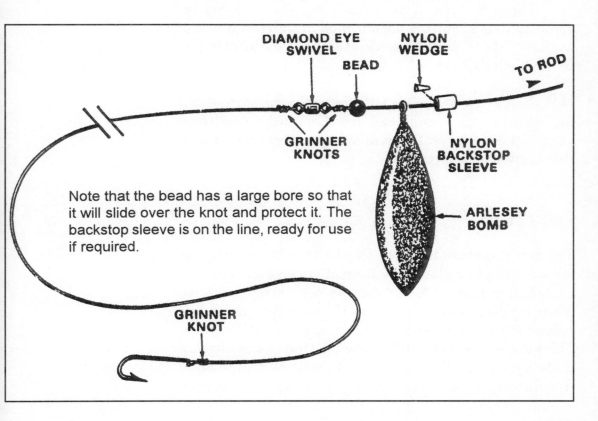

DIAMOND EYE SWIVEL

NYLON WEDGE

BEAD

TO ROD

GRINNER KNOTS

NYLON BACKSTOP SLEEVE

Note that the bead has a large bore so that it will slide over the knot and protect it. The backstop sleeve is on the line, ready for use if required.

ARLESEY BOMB

GRINNER KNOT

Not all that many anglers realise just how much resistance there can be between points D and F in Fig.41, by virtue of rod ring friction and bobbin climber arrangements especially when the latter are wet and dirty from splashed mud. Keep them clean.

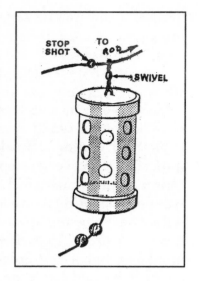

Left: Fig.43.

It is easy to see why indication at point D is far more sensitive, hence the arrival of spring, swing and quiver-tip techniques.

This conveniently leads me to state the obvious. Wherever a bomb is used while legering, it can be interchanged with a suitable swimfeeder from the excellent range now available.

They, in turn, have interchangeable weights on some models including the addition of shot to a line link as shown above. In extreme cases a small bomb can be put in the feeder's base.

Note: Never use a leger rig with the backwind stop switch on together with a closed bail-arm. Eventually you'll lose your rod unless you fish with a baitrunner type of reel, that is switched to runner.

Leger Rods

The older rods tended to be shorter than those available now, a two piece glass fibre from about eight feet to nine and a half feet long. Modern composite or carbon versions, often supplied with a selection if spiggoted quiver-tips extend to about ten feet or even eleven and a half feet long. There are even some with intermediate rod-pieces offering a choice of lengths on the same rod! Whether these developments are just sales gimmicks or genuine developments that will prove useful tools for specific jobs remains to be seen. The longer, modern versions with an action best described as a long tip action are welcome, as far as I'm concerned. The added length certainly adds to casting control and much better fish-playing characteristics. These feeder and quiver rods have a casting weight of about 40 grams, yet despite all that, I do own a carbon quiver tip of ten foot length on which I have had good bags of chub - and I have a superb rod with the famous Avon Mark IV through action, which is so flexible, in many chubbing situations, the use of a quiver becomes superfluous. It's a handmade 'special' by Nicholas Whipp of Nefyn, a craftsman if ever there was one!

Eight

THE QUARRY

Roach

The roach (*Rutilius Rutilius*) exists in such large numbers and in such a wide variety of waters of both poor and good qualities, that I cannot imagine a coarse angler who has not caught one. Their prolific breeding to a large extent prevents them from reaching maximum size in their maturity, especially in close waters. Despite their familiarity, a good roach is a fine fish. It sports silvery scales with a greenish, black back, red eyes and fins. The true roach can be distinguished from the dace by having a deeper body and fewer scales along its lateral lines; forty-four in the roach and forty-eight to fifty in the dace. This may be important as dace and roach occupy the same stretch of water. The front edge of their dorsal fin is in line with the base of the ventral fin, while the rudd's dorsal, for instance, is much farther back towards the tail.

The roach can be caught by all manner and means, the maggot being the most popular bait. Fine tackle is used in most cases, yet I cannot help feeling that it is the larger baits which would account for bigger specimens being caught. In my view, too, many anglers arrive after the sun has risen and depart when it has set, missing out on the larger brethren. Of course, you have to find a water in which they exist! Big roach have a small mouth, to be sure, but they still take bait of a generous kind. The head or tail of a lobworm will disappear quite easily, as will a large piece of bread flake. It is the sort of feeding big roach love. Put a maggot on a size twenty hook and you will come up with a small roach - one after the other.

I know that on most waters good sized roach do not exist. I also know how long you have to fish for a good sized roach, but to catch a specimen be prepared to use every skill you possess, as well as applying every tactic you know how. For big fish, of any kind, possess a degree of craftiness that leaves their lesser brethren amateurs.

I was recently on a water and had a fair number of roach to about 1½lb. An elderly, and one would have thought experienced, man was extracting roach of about ½lb. How was it, he wanted to know, was I avoiding myriad perch and roach of the same size? I had to look at his tackle and bait and found it to be immaculate. He was catching on maggot and caster. Mine were not specimens by any means but they were, as far as I know, the best in the water - and I was in with such a chance of a two-pounder! I was on sweetcorn on a size ten hook.

There are so many clones about using identical tackle and bait, that it sometimes pays to be different. Often, successful anglers who seek publicity, and there are many who do not you will find, do things a little differently from the rest, even if it is down to a different and larger bait.

Bream

On casual inspection the common or bronze bream (*Abramis Brama*) and the silver bream (*Blicca Bjoerkna*) up to about 1lb in weight, appear to be very alike. The colouring of both is, at that stage, silver. Closer examination reveals the marked differences. The eye diameter in relation to the length of the distance between eye and snout tip is the first indication to look for in trying to establish identification. The eye diameter/snout length from eye to snout tip on the common or bronze is greater, while on the silver it is smaller. The common bream has more than twenty rays in its anal fin, the silver less than twenty, while the common bream has fifty to sixty scales along its lateral lines. The silver bream has less than fifty.

Both species are slow growing fish, but when the silver reaches about 1lb in weight it ceases to grow at all and the common continues upwards into double figures.

Not only that, the common begins to change colour into maturity while the silver remains the silver it always was! The colour of maturing common bream gradually takes on an olive appearance, although the depth of shading differs from water to water and even between fish!

Having established all that, you might think that identification of mature bream, at least, was easy enough. So it would be, if it were not for the fact that they, like all silver bream, love to hybridise with their bream cousins, each with the other, and with other roach. As frequent back-crossing occurs, identification becomes complex, even though roach/bream hybrids do have deeper bodies than the true roach! In fact, only expert dissection can be relied upon to establish true identity, usually by inspection of the pharyngeal teeth. The angler, of course, may not be unduly concerned with such things, unless he is trying to establish a record fish weight.

Having implied that bream are habitual in their movements they seem to be apparently prone to change one set of habits for another, perhaps due to angling pressure, perhaps the explosion of various natural foods, it is hard to say. They may be more easily 'conditioned' by external factors than is realised; all of which is frustrating to the angler who by dedication and observation has spent some time in tracking down their patrol routes and feeding areas. After all, it cannot be expected of them to follow set paths indefinitely if the natural food simply dries up or they are continually facing the consequences of angling activity!

Unlike the tench, bream tend to travel high in the water when weed is dense and high, which may have several causes, one of which may be the need for clear relationships between them for shoaling purposes. They tend to be happier in their movements, going down in a relatively weed-free area to feed, rather like a clearing in a forest. If you can find such areas in a densely weeded water it is likely you have found a bream feeding area.

In the fenland drains of East Anglia, one of their traditional areas of habitat, the short session anglers looked for an area of cloudy water as an indication of bream feeding, for in such confined environments they have little choice but to travel up and down the miles of water, stopping only where they find food. In waters with featureless beds and little weed, especially if it is a very large water, it is very difficult indeed to ascertain their whereabouts at all, perhaps the pleasure angler only being likely to stumble across them accidentally, by chance! You could, given the time and opportunity, try to establish a feeding area by pre-baiting over a long period, but as the bream takes baits common to many other species such as lobworm, maggot and bread it is likely to become a regular spot for shoals of roach, perch, gudgeon and the like. Any free offerings have to be chosen to eliminate hoards of 'bits', unless you like catching them, that is!

Bream do seem to prefer larger baits than most fish, however, and the best feeding times are undoubtedly during the night, especially an hour or so either side of dawn and dusk.

Silver bream crop up in almost any still water nowadays and the pleasure angler may not be unduly elated at the capture of such a small fish. He is far more likely to prefer common bream. So it is the common or bronze bream on which I shall devote some space, for, despite the apparent disdain with which they are regarded by seekers of hard fighting fish, often referred to as 'snotty', (the fish, not the anglers), fishing for good bream is a pleasant way of spending time.

The Common Bream

It is, if judged by its body area alone, relatively light in weight, and as this fork-tailed fish is slow in growth, stocking policy is something of a long-term business. It is very much the specimen hunter approach that captures the large bream but even a laid back pleasure angler can come up with a few of medium size and over with little effort. They are not that difficult to catch but are very difficult to find. It is even more difficult to pin down feeding areas.

Bream are shoaling fish and are creatures of habit, so if the angler is well informed or has done his homework well, he is in a position to lay a groundbait 'trap' for them and, hopefully, be able to induce them to get their heads down and feed. If they do, by careful casting and retrieval he may take several more before they are satisfied with food or move on, for bream shoals are forever on the move, save in the height of summer when they love to bask in the sun, lazing at or near the surface. They are shy fish, sensitive to sound and vibration. They also possess good eyesight and, you will find that due to these characteristics daylight fishing for them is often a long distance affair, calling for legering techniques, unless the water is very narrow or very small.

There is an almost a universal belief that bream respond to heavy groundbaiting. Whether that is due to writer after writer unthinkingly saying so or to anglers who do so just because other anglers follow this pattern, I don't know. I, too, am certain they seem to love finding an area covered with an interesting mix of crumb and free offerings but I am equally sure they can be scared out of their wits by a barrage of groundbait 'bombs', given the shy and sensitive responses bream show to noises, vibration and sightings of man.

I've float fished for bream on the drains of East Anglia, some so narrow they can only patrol along its length and in passing remain well within casting distance. In such waters, finding a stretch of 'coloured' water is, for the short season pleasure angler, as much as you can do to find them. In wide waterways, on lakes and meres and on reservoirs, a paternoster or leger rig is more likely to reach them. Mature waters, including gravel pits, are likely to hold good bream. Indeed, record sized fish have been taken from the latter types of water in recent years.

Arriving at a weedy, clear watered pit last season I met, by chance, Jim Hindley, an all-round angler of some note. I was saved from many hours of investigation and observation by Jim who kindly pointed out an area of bream, a broad plateau at the centre of the water, a clearing in a veritable forest of surface high weed with which the rest of the pit was infested. The rig I used, shown in the picture of the bream, overcame the problems of casting over great banks of high weed onto the plateau and retrieving through them without tangling once.

The feeder used is designed to rise quickly on the retrieve, and certainly did so, skimming across thirty or forty yards of weed effortlessly.

Bream are not renowned for their fighting ability, for once they have struggled a bit, they give in and are easily drawn to the net if you hold them high in the water, their mouths just clear of the surface. They can, however, put up a considerable resistance on the line in the early stages of the fight by turning their broad bodies sideways to the line of pull and forming a cup shape, so, what with all the weed I plumped for line of 4½BS and encountered no problems.

Jim Hindley even moved out of his favourite swim because his stay was to be far longer than mine, just to give me the chance! There are not too many anglers about like that these days. We both took a few reasonable fish of between six and eight pounds. No doubt, had we fished through the night instead of in the day, we may have done better, but then we were both there for pleasure, and pleasurable it truly was!

Perch

The bold aggressive perch (*Perca Fluviatilis*) is a handsome fish, rugged in looks, sandpaper rough to the touch but prone to being easily damaged when carelessly handled. They often seem quick to go into shock and rather slow to recover. Its outline and colouring pattern is unique to British waters, whilst its demeanour is always that of a hunter, though a comparatively small one. Greyish vertical bars on the flanks and orangey red fins are not, in themselves, all that spectacular, but the dorsal fins and the large mouths certainly are, adding a dimension to this beautiful fish not found in any other of its size. The foremost dorsal is sail-like with spiny, sharp fin rays;

these to be wary of when handling, for they easily skewer the skin of the unwary. Its diet consists of various forms of live organisms, including the common angling baits, worms in particular, and as the perch grows it becomes totally carnivorous and even cannibalistic. A shoaling fish itself, it is never far from shoals of other small species such as the minnow and bleak which can often be seen in shallow water scattering in wild disarray as they try to escape the attack of a perch.

Such scenes may well have earned the perch the title of being the 'bovver-boy' of freshwater species. Yet, as it grows older and more solitary, it tends to lose its shoaling habits and become more pike-like in its predatory methods, lying in wait behind a tree root, in a gully, or well hidden in reed beds, any kind of cover, in fact, before erupting into an arrow like attack on an unwary victim, its acceleration and speed remarkable. It will attack again and again until its quarry is damaged and worn down by its dogged pursuit.

The perch feeds at lower temperatures, so it follows that in winter it is likely to follow quarry species down to deep water, often to the bottom of very deep still waters. Because of temperature changes it has to be sought at varying depths. The suspended paternoster rig shown in Fig.34 is a good method of finding them. There is some evidence from several experienced anglers that a perch when hooked is followed by its brethren towards the margin, thus dispersing a shoal, if one exists! My experience backs up this theory, from sighting other perch of about the same size moving after their unfortunate kin.

I personally think there is more chance of picking up really good sized perch in winter rather than summer, due to a lack of weed growth and the tendency to be nearer the bottom. In summer, a well-weeded gravel pit, full of bars and gullies, makes the catching of a big perch one of the hardest of angling achievements, unless it is out of sheer luck. In clear water, where its vision is unimpaired and its predatory feeding most successful, its colour deepens to richer tones and its weight can increase to record proportions. Such an old warrior can only be described as magnificent! At rest, the perch seems to be, in colour, shape and bearing, reminiscent of some Eastern ship, an exotic one, in full sail; or is it me who had a severe dose of the Flash Gordons when very young - or the *Nautilus* in submerged fantasy!

Without doubt, my favourite bait for the perch is the worm. The tail end of the lobworm seems to attract them, so when legering I inject the tail with air, making it buoyant so that it waves about enticingly, hooking it at the end. Putting the hook through once is enough. Always choose the liveliest worm because the perch relies heavily on its sight for food, as well as vibration, hence the success of a small spinner such as a Mepps. You can, however, attract them with a trout lure. In doing so, a black lure is the most effective, especially in winter.

If you know of a water that has big perch, fish the larger type of worm and following that I would put the minnow and gudgeon next on the list of priority baits, especially as the gudgeon remains active longer than most. Then come the small roach and rudd, in my book. Mind you, if you have a personal objection to live baits of any kind, you can always go for dead bait. For me, however, in comparison with the worm, spinner or trout lure, the dead bait is a non-starter.

Float fishing with worm isn't that much different. A buoyant worm held down with a shot on a hooklength in a similar way to the carp rig, as illustrated in Fig.32, does the trick. It is too soon to strike at perch the moment the float moves. Wait until the float has gone down. Hence, again, it is a matter of conscience in that there may be a risk of deep hooking. Be careful this does not happen, cutting the line and drawing the hook out through the gill cover, if necessary - and if possible, without damaging the fish. Large perch are rare enough as it is!

One of the snags in fishing for big perch, either by spinning or by fishing a livebait, is that you are likely to catch a pike. With me it was the other way round, very early in my fishing years. I caught a record perch! A perch of 5lb plus weight!

Carp

The crucian carp (*Carassius Carassius*) is one of the carp families without barbels. Compared to the common carp (*Cyprinus Carpio*) it is a small fish, one of 2lbs or 3lbs being a good one. The crucian is deeply bodied, a golden brown colour and is much more tolerant of cold and of poor water conditions than its superior sized cousin. It feeds mainly on small invertebrates and is usually fished for with small live baits such as maggot and worm but can be caught on small cheese cubes or cheese paste. It is a timid feeder, and takes a bait tentatively and timorously. Therefore, fine, light tackle is the order of the day, presented delicately. This being so, it is as well it lacks the strength and fight of the common carp!

Cyprinus Carpio is quite another story. Even at a tender age its power and zip foretell its fighting potential, the young common carp being particularly ferocious in this respect. It is thought to have been introduced to this country long ago by monks who bred them for the table. Indeed, in some continental countries they are still regarded as something of a delicacy. The origins of different breeding strains of carp are, to some extent, lost in the mists of time. Suffice to say, breeding programmes have diversified their shape somewhat, as well as changing scale patterns and scale size from the classic common carp's normal scaling. Breeding in controlled conditions produces a fast growing and heavy fish with a few large scales, and in some instances, no scales at all, the result being an economical fish for the table. I doubt if anyone could have foreseen the growth of such fish eventually sparking off such an interest among anglers in this country and, subsequently, abroad.

Modern carp angling is so well documented and discussed in a plethora of books and periodicals devoted to it, that it is best to refer the interested reader towards those societies based in Britain dedicated to the carp angler and his interests. Addresses for the same are given at the back of this book.

Above: Mini boilies on hair rig.
Below: Rolling boilies.

Above: A Cardinal 55 reel - no longer on the market.
Below: Twin carp rods.

Above: An Angler catapulting boilies.
Below: An Angler with an old-fashioned carp rod.

Above: Common carp.
My daughter shows how it's done!

Keepnet used in fast water. Ribble fishing - bad practice.

Returning carp to water.

Female angler float fishing.

An old-fashioned carp rod and reel.

Above: Angler fishing winter.
Below: An Angler with mirror carp.

Above: Landing a carp.
Below: An Angler using a swing-tip rod. Note the board aiding bite registration.

Above: Angler fishing river.
Below: Angler with mirror carp.

Above: Angler float fishing.
Below: Robin at maggot box.

Above: Angler float fishing on the Calder River.
Below: A selection of waggler and joggler floats.

Holiday angler float fishing for roach and tench. Second rod for carp at Lowfields, Lincs.

Ten foot rod with spring tip for chub and barbel.

Angler with float and leger rods out.

Angler going for tench.

A better tench.

A good spot on the River Ribble for chub and dace.

Above: Chub catch.
Below: A good haul of chub, dace and roach.

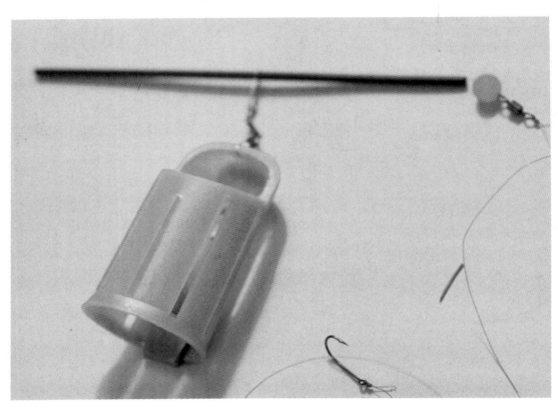

Above: The leger rig mentioned in text for fishing through weed and getting the bream.
Below: A good 7lb bream.

Above: A near leather and a linear mirror carp.
Below: A common carp.

Above: Small perch as a live bait for pike.
Below: The best part of the day! The fish think so anyway!

The Common Carp

The 'root' form of *Cyprinus Carpio*, the common carp, has a pair of barbels, a long dorsal fin and is, unlike other forms of the species, fully scaled, the scales regular, comparatively small and neat. It is not generally known by pleasure anglers that the mirror carp, the leather carp and the linear mirror are variations of common carp, the name 'common' being applied by popular usage to the 'root' strain. The mirror carp has a random scattering of large scales, the linear mirror, as the name suggests, has a line of large scales running from gill covers to tail, either adjacent to the dorsal or nearer the lateral line of the fish, while the leather carp has no scales at all in its 'pure' form.

The colours of all these varieties of fish differ a great deal, not only from water to water, but also from fish to fish, the predominant colours being, perhaps, shades of bronze and yellowish gold. The fully scaled mirror carp is a very rare and particularly beautiful fish, with mirror sized scaling in a regular pattern all over the body.

Due to the relatively short periods of warm weather in this country, and thus annual shorter feeding periods, the carp here are noticeably slower in growth and so are lighter than their continental brethren except in exceptional circumstances where the water condition, abundant food and their origin provide the exception, Redmire Pool being the best known of such waters. The book, *Redmire Pool*, by Len Arbery and Kevin Clifford, published by Beekay, is very well worth a read if your interest lies in such phenomena, or that pool's extraordinary history.

Weights in this country top the forty pound mark in some cases, but the highest known weight is in excess of fifty pounds. Even so, thirties are relatively rare with twenty pounders being present in enough numbers for most anglers to be in with a chance of picking one up, if they diligently seek out where they exist.

All carp fishing is exciting in its own way, it often being a fact that your younger, smaller carp sometimes put up a better fight than bigger ones, although stories of massive fish on the continental mainland towing anglers round in boats are common enough. One thing is certain; to fish for carp with inadequate tackle is folly, the risks of leaving hooks in fish being high. They *can* be caught on light rods and tackle with luck and not a little skill, but to be armed with rods of at least one and a quarter pounds TC and a line of six or seven pounds breaking strain is about as light as I would go, and then only in snag free swims.

Hooks usually range between about size ten up to size two, dependent on the type of bait, the type of rig and the balancing of bait. Strong forced hooks are a necessity, while all hooks, lines and knots should be examined regularly and tested to ensure maximum reliability. Many anglers do not realise that hooks, even very sharp ones, do not always penetrate fully on the strike, but bite deeper as the fish is played. Watch out, too, for carp with softer mouths than usual, the hook having a tendency to tear out of its hold, such fish usually inhabiting waters with soft, silty bottoms.

There is a fascination about carp angling which cannot be denied. It is a fish that provokes a dedication among anglers which is not only attributable to the size of the fish and its fighting power. It is a form of angling surrounded by its own brand of mystery and it has its own unique history, linked to that angling sage and writer, Richard Walker, who, with his friends, set out to catch what were until then regarded as *uncatchable* fish. He succeeded with the capture of the British record fish, Clarissa, at 44lbs, a feat indeed in the 1940s.

Whether the surge of interest in carp fishing is due to Walker himself, his friends, Redmire Pool history - from where Clarissa was taken - or from the fish itself, it is hard to say. A combination of all those things, I'm sure, but take off it did, until now, at the start of the 90s it is still the fastest growing arm of coarse fishing.

The pleasure angler may well have access to water holding carp, and large ones at that. More and more waters are being stocked with them, especially holiday type venues. Such venues advertise the fact and to some extent depend on carp to draw in customers, so the holidaymaking angler should be prepared to deal with them. There is always a chance carp will respond to simple baits such as worm, maggot and bread, even though a great deal is said about complex carp boilies and specials. Ready made boilies are freely available now in most tackle shops so the casual angler may well succumb to the lure of the carp - and I have to say, should he by chance catch a good one, he is likely to be hooked himself!

Before he is, he should have some idea of exactly what he is letting himself in for if he wishes to be consistently successful in carp fishing, if you measure success by the size of the fish caught! It demands of the participant a dedication bordering on fanaticism with good tackle, usually highly priced as are the myriad sundry needs of the camper-out, for if the carp you seek are far from home, the need to stay out on the bank for day and nights on end is required to make fishing trips worthwhile!

Eventually, the need to pay high prices to fish exclusive waters can arise and a great deal may have to be sacrificed to pay that price - and not only in monetary terms! The intrepid would-be carp maestro also has to be a thinking angler, for whilst carp are not brainy in our terms, they do have a sensitivity and natural cunning that leads men to pit their acumen in a never ending battle of wits. You also need to have a lucky streak, as all anglers do, no matter what their level of expertise may be. A prime example was Richard Walker himself who, when his record fish fell to his line, was fishing an identical bait in an identical manner a few feet away from his friend. History is wrought with such chance!

The greatest innovation in modern times must surely be the hair-rig, a device so simple, like all good ideas, that one has to ask why no-one ever thought of it before Kevin Maddocks and Len Arbery? Well, they probably did, but nobody had applied it to carp fishing! In some waters carp are learning to avoid that particular trap, and alternative means have been devised to trap carp into a take, mainly by making the bait and hook behave in the same way as a free offering. So the battle of human wit against the natural cunning of carp continues apace.

Basic Principles

The ways of fixing a hair to a hook are shown in Figs.12-13; from the bend, from the eye and from a point midway between the eye and bend. In the latter case, the hair is secured to the eye and a small piece of silicon rubber is slid up from the eye to trap the hair in the desired position. The length of hair in all cases is variable, dependent on the manner in which the fish react. In the water I fish it is rarely necessary to have it more than one inch long and is often tied very close to the hook, so picked up, or sucking up, the bait means the hook is taken with it. A popular method is to make the bait and hook buoyant by various means. The insertion of polystyrene into the hard bait is one way. The bait and hook are then anchored by a single shot, as in Figs. 11-12. Obviously, the hookbait is then made easily visible and the carp takes in the bait against resistance of only one shot. Adjust buoyancy and shotting weight until the bait only just sinks slowly, the slower the better! If you can, achieve exactly a neutral buoyancy, and many anglers use diverse methods to achieve that, some of which are shown in detail in Andy Little's book, *Big Carp Fishing*, published by The Angler's Mail. It also shows, again in detail, ways to affix baited hairs to various rigs. Such publications - and there are many - will prove invaluable to the angler who is setting out on his first carping adventure.

One of my own rigs is shown in Fig.44, as a means of allowing a minimum of resistance in the initial stages of the bite before the fish moves off and is 'shocked' into a run. It is effective in places where carp is moving from place to place, feeding as they go, so that only a small amount of free offerings need accompany such a rig. A great mass of such would keep them confidently occupied in a tight area.

Sliding Rig

I thought up this rig for waters where carp were becoming wary of the resistance involved in long range legering. Once the PVA string has dissolved and the bomb is not moved the hooklength is virtually a free line! It works, too, but the slip ring needs to be strong and the knots checked regularly in case of wear and tear.

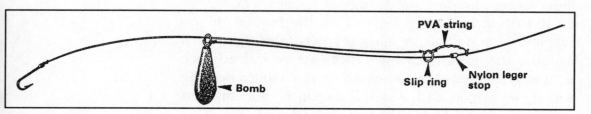

Above: Fig.44. One of the author's own rigs.

Pike

Esox Lucius, the pike, is likely to cause extremes of feeling in anglers. The pike lover, usually a specialist, may well be captivated by this powerful predator, while at the other extreme, those who dislike pike or even positively hate them, other than the game angler who has a seemingly valid reason for his dislike in that the pike may harry, damage or kill his own beloved species, whether they be trout or salmon, could not give a logical reason for their dislike of the fish or their complete indifference to its fate or well-being.

The days when pike would automatically be clubbed to death, or left to die on the bank, are fast receding, as even the most unthinking or uncaring types are becoming aware of the interdependence of all species and that the extinction of any species would be a tragedy.

Anglers as a body have always cared about the angling environment and in these days of green propaganda and green politics every facet of angling is becoming more and more conservation minded. Pike lovers are now teaching the correct ways of handling pike and returning them unharmed to the water.

The pike is unmistakable in appearance. Long and

slender, its eyes set high in the head, underslung jaws full of sharp teeth, its dorsal fin set far back near the tail, it does have a fearsome look about it, as much due, perhaps, to the mental images correlated to the shark. It's certainly built for speed, if only in short predatory bursts, and given the right conditions in regard to food availability and quality, it can grow to a great size. Pike are predatory, even at a tender age. That being so, the obvious way to catch them is to present live or dead fish baits or to spin for them using imitation fish, plugs or spoons. The live or dead baits are usually legered on the bottom or are suspended midwater by various paternoster rigs which includes the use of very buoyant floats, or indeed such baits may be floated out across the water using a floating end rig equipped with a sail. It should be remembered that the bait might well be a salt water dead fish such as a piece of herring or mackerel, flavoured with fish oil and other attractions.

Pike have a tendency to congregate at the junction of inflowing streams and rivers where they join lakes or ponds. In fact, river born pike are extremely ferocious when caught. Rather than dash about chasing prey thus wasting precious energy they are likely to wait in weed or rush, their mottled appearance affording them excellent camouflage.

The pike-perch or Zandor, again is loved or hated, the latter due to the belief of its effect in the cyprinus population. Easily recognised by its two dorsal fins, the foremost being the smaller, its introduction to the lowlands of Cambridge has resulted in rapid distribution in the East Anglia area. Small fish are the best bait, and tackle need not be so tough as that used for pike. Wire hook traces, for example, are not necessary.

Chub

Leuciscus Cephalis is a denizen of the rivers. It's another member of the carp family, rarely found in still waters and when it is, it is hard to catch. The fins are reddish, the anal and dorsal being convex, unlike the dace. It is similar to the other whose anal fin is concave. Where chub are found is often the place where barbel are too. Large, older chubs are predatory, so they can be taken on the fly and small spinner. In fact, they can be taken on a wide variety of baits such as worm breadflake or paste, whilst luncheon meat, sweetcorn and maggots will also tempt this handsome and accommodating fish.

One good method I have enjoyed is to wade out to the middle of a river, to a fast stretch of water and from there allow a ball of sausage meat to find its way to a quieter chubby pool and fished free line. In summer they frequent shallow water, where they can be seen basking while in winter they find deep holes from which they can be legered. Where circumstances allow, it is common practice to use swimfeeder technique and a quivertip rod action.

The chub is a shy fish and stalking becomes necessary, especially when float fishing. However, the chub flourishes during winter when the weather is often so cold that the line freezes to the rod. A way to prevent this is to apply a few drops of glycerine to the rod rings. The chub is often found hidden beneath floating vegetation or even an overhanging bank. Anything that floats at all may hide chub.

Barbel

The barbel (*Barbus Barbus*) is perhaps as easily recognised as the perch, in its own way, having two sets of barbels, one at the snout and one set at the back of the mouth. It's a sleek torpedo of a fish which fights all the way to the net. It is likely to inhabit the middle reaches of a river and it loves to lay up in holes close to fast water, and behind stones and logs. It particularly likes gravelly bottoms on which thick weedbeds flourish. The dorsal fin is concave and pointed, as is the upper part of its forked tail. It is catholic in its taste, taking a wide variety of food, as is the chub, and it can be fished for in the same manner. It is a fish that can be drawn towards a swim with a trickle of free groundbait running through the water, rather than a great dollop all in one go! If loose offerings are fed into the swim in as natural a manner as is possible - both before and during fishing - barbel can be drawn right up to the hookbait. If chub are present, too, you are likely to come up with a few of these before you hit a barbel, but when you do the wait will be worthwhile. Such is the fight of the barbel, he is likely to be exhausted by the time he is landed. Great care is required in handling and returning fish to the water, and sometimes a little patience may be required in holding the fish upright in the water before allowing it to swim off under its own steam.

They can be found in such rivers as the Avon, Ribble, Trent, Stour, Ouse, Thames and Severn, all of which are, in parts, relatively fast flowing and wide. The barbel grows well into the double figures, giving exceptional sport to any angler.

Tench

The tench (*Tinca Tinca*) varies from a light yellowish green through shades of greeny olive to black. It is easily recognised with its tiny scales covered in a slippery, but not unpleasant, mucus and its red eyes. It is a fighter of a fish, usually putting up a good fight all the way to the net. It has a broad powerful tail with a deep 'wrist' while its fins tend to be rounded. It also has a powerful pair of barbels. Tench are lovers of weedy, muddy and preferably deep water, rich in all manner of aquatic invertebrates, but it can be readily conditioned to eat man-made foods.

In recent years there has been a massive increase in tench weights, rising to low double figures, especially when full of spawn. Female tench are much prized by anglers as they are a good deal larger than the male, the latter's ventral fin being more pointed. Bloated in this situation of spawning they lose something of their aesthetic beauty, for me, but there is no denying the joy of an angler having caught such a monster. At one time a 5lbs fish was considered a good one. Now, in many waters, such a fish is considered commonplace. Weights from 6lbs upwards are considered average by tench specialists with weights of 7lbs, 8lbs, 9lbs and upwards being the norm, and double figure fish always being on the cards. One theory being put forward is the introduction of protein rich carp boilies. Another reason is the seepage of farm fertiliser into waters that is said to enrich them. A great deal is said about fertilizer seepage....but it's an ill wind...

Strangely, although there has been an increase in the weight of other species, the dramatic increase in tench weight seems to be unique. River tench do not seem to be affected. Anyone who is interested can find an in-depth study of the situation in Len Arbery's book, *Catching Big Tench*, published by David and Charles.

The classic method of catching tench is by raking a swim. The disruption caused by repeatedly dragging a rakehead through the water releases a myriad of life forms from the mud, silt, weed and debris. This attracts tench rather than frightens them away. Such raking can be carried out immediately prior to fishing, with good effect. Evening, through night to early morning, is said to be the best time to fish for tench, but I have caught them at all times of the day and in a wide variety of conditions and weathers. Misty, moist early mornings with tench rolling close to weed beds, tiny bubbles exciting great interest and anticipation at times have been disappointing, while I have taken them in the heat of a midsummer afternoon in large gobbets of sausage meat paste from a shallow, featureless pool, on single sweetcorn on inky black nights, the weather being storm turbulent, wind and rain lashing my face. I've caught them also on carp flavoured baits and on my favourite bait, bread. There is little doubt that the best time for tench is early in the new season, for they very quickly learn to avoid noise and vibration set up by bank pressure and quickly learn how to avoid rigs and baits. Colder weather sends them into hibernation later in the season when they may well bury themselves in the mud, though a mild spell will often result in a fish.

I prefer a rod with a soft action when playing tench, especially on the float, because such a rod helps to absorb the shocks and plunges of a surging fish. Nowadays, I use line of about 4lbs breaking strain with a hooklength being as soft and pliable as possible, Multistrand or Kryston's Silkworm being ideal. While investigating a bait, the tench, having a broad and powerful tail, is quite capable of moving float - and bait - away! So I am tempted to keep the float in-situ by laying on or by use of a float leger.

Another method I favour when facing the wind with a steepish margin is to waggler fish, allowing the float rig to slowly drift in towards me, taking care to mend the line all the time. I am convinced the tench is a fish that follows wind direction looking for food, so I literally comb the bottom, using a buoyant waggler allowing the float to drift towards me naturally. It can be argued that the undertow is against natural presentation here, but I am trying to find hotspots where food debris occurs naturally. I know of one old claypit in which I found it well nigh impossible to catch tench in any other way, even if the method is a bit crude and does not follow theory. But then, tench cannot read.

Below: Fig.45.

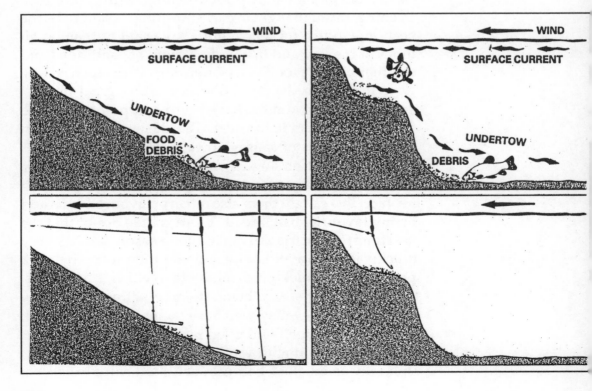

Using a slider waggler, the depth setting can be altered at will, quickly dealing with dramatic depth settings. As the indicator is close to the hook, the float disappears without warning, the fish having little option but to turn away from the angler in such cases, perhaps diving deeper.

In some cases you may find the tench will rise in the water to very narrow ledges, sometimes close to the angler, so it is best to find a tree or bush - even if it does not exist, make a home-made screen! If the water is ruffled or choppy, refraction will help enormously; even so it is best if one is stealthy and quiet.

Rod, Pole Or Perch

One rod, pole or perch is a phrase from arithmetic tables that has a lilting ring to it, I always think. It rolls off the tongue with nursery-rhyme charm. It also has, for me, connotations with the delightful art of angling.

Now, as anyone knows me will tell you, I am not an out and out numbers-man, although many have been the pressures in life to try and convert me. One of the first to try was a long, tall and thin 'Chalkie' in a black gown at school, who would leap up and down like a demented Dracula, gibbering what was, to me, algebraic gobble-de-gook; while I would while away the time filling in all the noughts on the front cover of a grubby exercise book or gaze in wonderment at the not inconsiderable tidemark on Nellie Kettleworth's neck. I was sure that teacher was an agent of the Devil sent to torment the likes of me!

Long since left to my own devices, I would daydream the boring hours away as I watched dust-motes dancing in the rays of sun that pierced the gloom of that stifling room. That sun, I would muse, was shining down on arable fields where a scattering of Lincolnshire souls toiled to extract a living from the Fenland. They worked alongside great hairy-legged shire horses whose affinity with soil and toil was only matched by their affinity with the men who rode them home at dusk. In time out from school we would watch them come as we sat and fished the long, straight waterways; roads and drain, side by side, forming a grid on the flat landscape.

The men rode side-saddle on those broad backs, the leather traces now loosely gathered to hang from the horse collar, the riders swaying with the slow, ponderous gait, reminiscent of the mahout on India's beasts of burden. That way, they could view the water from on high, raising an arm in cheery greeting to each angler as they went by, plodding, unhurried, sure and strong. Sometimes they would call out from their lofty perch, "Any luck, boy?"

Each angler according to his temperament would answer by word or sign. If the catch was moderate, the number of fish was shouted back, while a particularly good catch often resulted in short nets of knotted green string being hauled out and held triumphantly aloft as living proof of their angling prowess - and some would shake disconsolate heads.

Those men and horses seemed to symbolise the ever-constant nature of Fenland life. We were not to know a tide of change would sweep the horse away, and many a man, too; that mechanical elephants in efficient majesty would take their place - that crops and waters would be subject to chemicals sprayed from the air!

In those days, lark, seagull, pheasant, crow and lapwing ruled the air - until the shadow of hawk flitted over the land. Humped-back bridges strode the drains, under which we would hide from sun and rain and hope to catch a perch from the damp, brick caverns, while the sounds of hooves overhead were amplified into hollow clopping, the horse resting momentarily on the brow for the man to gaze down the long ribbon of water below - though they had seen that view a thousand times before. Perhaps they remembered their own boyhood days when gangs raked the mud-lined drains for eels, taking them to the village communal copper-pot so that the villagers might ease their hunger with eel and potato soup, staving off the gnawing emptiness of empty bellies until better times came. For we had heard of winters so hard a man could skate from the edge of the Wolds, where Hobhole Drain began, to Boston market! As they looked along the water, maybe, those sons of toil reflected how life was now good.

One rod, pole or perch equals 5½ yards: one of the few facts I could remember from the endless lists of Tables, even though, to me, it was a particularly useless fact. Looking today in metric conversion tables - no-one can avoid numbers forever - I see it says "The rod, pole or perch is now obsolete."

"Really!" Well, there's still plenty of rods about; the pole is here to stay, that's for sure; and the perch? It did almost become obsolete, as did the shire horse, but in the case of the perch, hopefully, it is now making a comeback!

Pray with me to the gods of fishdom it returns to its former glory, because it never seemed to matter whether it was large or small, a perch was somehow special.

Gathered along the banks of Hobhole, Bellwater or Thorpe Culvert, escapees from 1066 and all that, we fished many a happy day away. We had left behind our tiny stream, for now, with bikes, we could tackle Big Fish Country!

The styles were simple enough; but the tackle rarely stood up to big fish when we hooked them. Limited finance denied us the variety of line strength and a range of hooks, and limited skills robbed us of many a fish. Landing nets were unknown to our gang. A bit of a cane rod, perhaps, an apology of a reel, a few shot, a home-made crow quill float painted in gaudy colours, two or three short draw hooks, a tin of worms - and you were in!

Whenever a fish was caught there was excitement; an infectious glee and pleasure from a shared experience. Much cavorting and shouting announced a successful strike! Group therapy had nothing, but nothing to teach those who knew such simple pleasures!

Roach, bream and eels responded to the humble worm, as well as the occasional gudgeon or Miller's Thumb. (Dear God, the struggles we had with eels! And once we found an eel head in a hessian sack on the banks of Hobhole Drain. The severed head alone filled the width of the sack. We could only guess who'd left it there and what its original size might have been! Inwardly, we hoped never to catch such a mammoth eel. It was in imagination of such frightening proportions, surely it would have dragged a small boy into the depths of the Drain, never to be seen again!)

The bream, it was found, responded well to a "sophisticated" ground-bait of chicken meal and mashed pig-potatoes, though as often as not when a good one came it broke your tackle.

If you caught a gudgeon, well, you tried to show

disdain, but the secret pleasure was there as you added one more to your keepnet. I mean, at the end of the day, if you hadn't caught the biggest fish, you might well have the most, if none had wriggled free through the knotted mesh of the net, that is!

But if and when a large-mouthed perch swallowed your worm the cry went up, "It's a perch!"

Everyone would gather to view a perch, irrespective of its size - for perch were, somehow, special. Maybe it was the colouring alone that made it so. Or perhaps it was the sandpaper texture of its body. Maybe its shape and markings. More likely, it was the perch commanded respect by virtue of having two dorsal fins; one a majestic fan of spiky fin on which it was easy to prick the hand on its spikes. Or was it the fascination of being able to gaze down its great gob at the blood-red gills pumping away in desperation. Invariably the hook was well down past the grinning lips, so accommodating is the perch to young anglers. It's a fish that does not muck about like tentative roach or finicky bream and tench. When it decides to take a worm, it takes it with gusto; the float keeps on going - down! Schoolboy strikes connect every time!

I remember the touch of regret when a small roach or gudgeon died in the keepnet and the sorrow when a bream was in distress, but somehow the death of a perch, even a small one, left you with a sense of guilt, an uneasy conscience.

One rod, pole or perch. Ay, what memories it evokes. Old stripey! Perca fluviatilis, as the letter-crunchers call it. Even a picture of a perch, a good drawing, can bring me back to a style of fishing I loved. Relaxed, carefree, joyful angling I find difficult to describe. It's not the water, nor is it nostalgia alone, for I've caught many a perch in many places, many times in the intervening years: and it has never failed to please. Silently, inside me, the cry goes up, "It's a perch!" In any case, I recall a perch to cap them all!

Not all that long ago, I was idly looking through my angling library when I came across the old Record Freshwater Fish List. Now, as I've explained, I'm not a numbers man but any kind of reading connected with fishing is okay by me. Naturally, my eye fell on the verification of Dick Walker's 44lb carp. And there she was, though now dead, living on, lying in state, as it were, in the annals of angling history. Now you and I and, indeed, Dick Walker himself may have felt a touch of sorrow for a certain Chris Yates who subsequently had a much larger fish disqualified from the original list, and, as you will see, I know a little how he must have felt!

Facts, as the number-crunchers of this world are fond of saying, are facts.

In the same list, out of the corner of my eye, I saw Perch, Perca fluviatilis - 4lb 12oz. Funny thing is, I had never known the record for perch before. Official rod caught weight... 4lb 12oz. Bells rang in my ears. Lights flashed before my eyes and my flabber was well and truly gasted! The awful truth hit home and my mind tried to grapple with the facts - and for a time failed. Hot Gossip were on the telly - and I took no notice!

At length, I lay back in my chair and closed my eyes. I relived the Great Perch Robbery! I saw again with a clarity of inner visions, back on the banks of Hobhole Drain as a lad, The Saga of The Big Perch and The Bicycle.

I was about ten years old at the time. Now, in truth, I cannot remember exactly what time of year it was, though it was hot and sunny. Nor could I swear to the time of day, but I was hungry. But I do remember where it was!

It was four pegs down from Three Bridges, where Bellwater links with Hobhole; that old venue where Sheffielders played havoc with the bream. Pouring out of the early morning 'fisherman's train', they would come - race is a better description - heedlessly hurrying down steep banks with the attendant risk of sliding into the water on slippery rye-grasses. The guttural curses and the rattle of tackle baskets told of their escape from the smoke and grime of Steel City.

Come to think of it, it must have been midweek on the red letter day of the BIG perch. Other than myself and two other lads, there was only one angler in sight. He was an old man with grey bushy eyebrows and a wide smile. Our antics amused him all day, I saw! Funny how some details stand out in the memory like that while others fade into the mists of forgetfulness. This incident, however, will never fade. I don't know an angler who forgets a really big fish!

We had cycled from the edge of the flatlands along Hobhole to Three Bridges. To young boys, it always seemed an eternity pedalling the last stretch, for the drain and road ran on in front of you mile after mile, unbroken except for the occasional humpbacked bridge. Great temptation overwhelmed at the first single bridge. We always dismounted to survey the prospects and deliberated the wisdom of fishing there or pushing on. This day it was to be Three Bridges, the decision made in the conscious knowledge that after the end of a tiring day it would be a long haul home on our half-size bikes, terminating in a steep uphill climb!

It was standard practise in those days for adults to fish one rod in hand and have a pike line staked to the bank nearby. A secret raid on my Dad's tackle-box had provided the thick, braided line, a treble hook and a bung float that would not have been out-of-place as a buoy on the Mersey. A roach was staked out live to hang about six inches below the float and left to its own devices. I hurled it as best I could, close to a weed bed, and unable to find a suitable stake, I secured it to my bike which lay halfway down the steep banking. Never much good at geometry and such, I assumed the anchorage safe and secure. It didn't dawn on me that a slippery incline and a direct pull of line at the same angle would allow even a small pike to take my bike into the water!

We had fished for hours, a few roach, gudgeon and a skimmer or two were in the keepnet, while the old man, I remember, smiled on and on. I don't think he caught much, but he didn't seem to mind. He was just happy to be there!

Suddenly, out of the blue, there was a hell of a commotion on the pike line. It was thrashing the water, and the bike, I saw, was gradually slithering down the bank!

Now, when you're young, there's a tendency to

wander as you fish, frequently casting in different areas of water. It is regarded by adults as a sign of immaturity and impatience - unless you are an adult. Then it's called stalking, or working a swim. Whatever the cause, I was a good fifty yards from the bike, the pike-line behaving as though a demented coot had grabbed at the roach.

I realise now, of course, that had the bike actually entered the water, it's not likely to have gone much farther, but then, with a panic bordering on sheer terror, I imagined an enormous pike of shark-like proportions dragging the bike into a terrible depth from which it would never return! I ran as fast as I could along the edge of the water and anyone who knows such banks will appreciate it is a tightrope act to move at such a speed there. Then, as often happens in cases of emergency, everything went into a kind of slow-motion; and I can relive it again now as though it were yesterday.

In this particular dream state - or nightmare, I was alone. A sort of time-warp took over as my mind began to consider the awful implications, even as I ran. I felt every footfall give a shock to my body as it fell, the shot-box rising and falling in my trouser pocket, those short grey ones we used to wear, my heart pumping faster as young adrenalin flowed, yet the gap twixt me and the bike seemed to close, oh, so slowly. I even remember stumbling, fighting for balance, regaining it, and forging on, as in my mind a mixture of fear and excitement vied for my attention. Excitement at the thrill of hooking a mighty pike, the fear of losing my beloved bike - and Dad's tackle! I lived a conversation in the future, already trying to work out the most plausible excuses.

"Where have you been 'till this time?"

"Hobhole."

"Do you know what time it is? I thought I said to be home by six?"

"I..I had to walk back, Dad. I lost my bike."

"Lost it! How on earth did you manage that?"

"A fish pulled it in."

I remember thinking as I ran, what a stupid excuse! But there it was happening now! And then would come the take, and his tackle had gone - I'd been in his box and.....

I got there just in time, the small wheels just entering the water. I grabbed the thrashing line and hauled hand over hand. Now I must admit, memory fades here, for the next thing I remember is looking at the most beautiful fish I had ever seen, let alone caught. Not only that, it was a perch! It was a Big perch!

My mates, who had wandered off farther than I, were arriving. "It's a perch!", I shouted in triumph. "It's a perch!"

"It's a big 'un, too", said the old man. In the excitement I had realised he had approached, too. I looked up at him. "Well done, lad, well done!" I remember him saying. For a moment I was transfixed by his bushy eyebrows and I could see why he was always smiling. He had a set of false teeth too big for his mouth. His lips simply were not large enough to cover them up!

As vivid as that memory is, I do not recall much after that until I walked into our house with my prize. My mother was baking, cakes, tart and pies. There were pans and flour everywhere. Dad was reading the Daily Herald. Mother was always baking and Dad was always reading the paper it now seems to me in retrospect.

Suitably impressed, they gathered round to admire The Big Perch. "That's a good 'un," Dad said. Mam grimaced, as much to say, don't bring your fish near my baking, but I knew, despite her negative grunt, she was pleased for me.

"A good 'un," I thought, "it's gigantic!" The decision was made to weigh it on the old brass-faced baking scales. It was made clear that if her precious scale-pan was to be used, I was going to have to wash it afterwards.

Now, as I've been to some length to make clear, I am not a numbers man, but even then I could count to ten, and I've always remembered one rod, pole or perch, yet to this day, I can clearly see that perch and the scale pointer swinging round to stop a fraction after the FIVE mark! Just over five pounds of perch is a thing to see, I can tell you - especially when you're only ten - and you've caught it!

The years passed by, and whenever I see a perch, or even a good picture of one, those memories return, much as I've told it here. A little voice inside me cries out, 'It's a perch!' and I see it all again.

Not until browsing down that old record list did I realise I had the makings of a record-holder.

This is a true story, and I'm not detracting from the listed record-holder in any way at all. I expect he caught his on conventional tackle. You see, I didn't use a rod, or a pole, for that matter. But I did have that perch. Unfortunately, the rules do not allow fish caught on a bicycle! And, you know, it was the true weight. The four undigested minnows fell out of its mouth into the kitchen sink before the fish was weighed!

The One That Got Away

A strong, warm wind blew unimpeded across the flat Dutch landscape, whipping up white-horses on the canal in front of me. To the left, the ribbon of undulating water was as straight as a die, its banks lined with reeds, now flattened by the rush of air. They danced wildly, kow-towing to the gale-force wind. Through slitted eyes I could just make out the dark block of sluice-gates foreshortening the horizon at that point. I could also see that there were several fences between the sluice and me. How many, I didn't know, for after the first two, perspective jumbled them all into one, leaving me to wonder how many fields were encompassed by their barbed symmetry.

The first field, I saw, had a herd of cows in it, lying down in a huddle, keeping a low profile. That ruled out scaling the fence. I had no intention of sharing my fishing with inquisitive bovine friends.

I dumped my rods, bedchair and haversack on the ground, relieved to be free of the weight, easing the ache in my neck and shoulders. To the right, about a half-mile away, the road bridge I had crossed spanned the water, and beyond that the canal curved out of sight. The heron sentinels had deserted their posts and no birds sang, or if they did the sound was torn away on the boisterous wind. I looked at the water and watched the fierce waves running towards the bridge with some trepidation. It was like looking at undulating grey soup with whipped cream on top!

I began to sort out fishing problems in my mind, when I saw the floating debris I was going to contend with. For a minute it didn't sink in until I saw the first island! It was sailing along majestically complete with reeds, flowered heads and stalks like car radio whip aerials. They passed me by with seeming indifference to my problems - problems their presence now compounded.

They were moving against the wind, for Pete's sake, and travelling at a fair rate of knots too! In reality, high water was being run off, I supposed, although for a moment I thought I was hallucinating.

So there it was - wind and waves running towards the bridge, the canal running off in the opposite direction through the sluice! With all the debris floating downstream, it would be impossible to have leger lines anywhere near the surface. I wondered how long the trailing roots of the weed islands were and could I get the lines low enough.

"No matter what, get your baits across to the opposite margin," had been the advice of local carp expert and exiled Brit, Barry Smith. Well, I'd give it a go, I decided. After all, that's what I'd gone for.

I looked at the floating Kon-Tikis with some trepidation, I can tell you, as I set up the first rod. If I couldn't hold a bait out there, I'd have to fish the near margin, that's all there was to it!

I aimed the rod slightly downstream at a bank indentation between two clumps of reed, imparting to the bomb as low a trajectory as I could. Fixed as a link-leger, I wanted the bomb to lodge in the soft mud, for conditions were such I doubted if bomb-weight alone would be enough. Smack, in it went, as much by good luck as fine judgement. I remember worrying if the bait was in the water or on the bank, so close was the bomb to the margin.

The rod was set at about forty-five degrees, the tip well down, hoping to avoid the line being picked up by trailing roots or sticks. I couldn't see the line, of course, and had to clip it tight. No sooner was that done and it flew out again, the Optonic sounder shrilling out its song. At first, I thought it was undertow or debris responsible, but it seemed to be paying out too fast for that, so I wound into what turned out to be a scraper twenty pound carp! After pumping it in against tow and weed-festooned line a short battle ended with it safely in the net. It all happened so quickly, I don't know who was the more surprised, the fish or me.

Thinking about it afterwards, that fish must have had a shock at being taken from the refuge it had obviously sought from the world of madness its underwater world had suddenly become, stopped in its tracks from dashing frantically towards the sluice and forced back upstream into the net!

I had visions of innumerable good carp lining the bank edge just waiting for me to drop a bait on their noses. At any rate, a lovely twenty pound common within a minute of the first cast augured will for the week's fishing holiday. It was not as easy as all that, of course, it rarely is, but three more came to the net in the next thirty-six hours, during which the wind died down and the undertow also slackened off to manageable proportions.

They were streamlined, big finned fish, immaculately scaled and beautifully golden. They were good solid fish, heavy for their size, but none reached the weight of the first. Without exception, they fled towards the sluice, putting up a great fight, as most commons do.

I think I should tell you I'm not a 'numbers man', as such. Size of fish alone is by no means the be all and end all of fishing for me. On the other hand, no-one can pretend size is unimportant. Every angler must hope for a really big fish someday. He may not talk of it, or even consciously accept the possibility, but the dream must be there! When on the continent, stories of continental monsters come to mind, and while Holland does have many more waters and more big fish than this country is likely to produce, it's not now listed high in the monster league. Its main appeal to me as a fishing paradise is not so much fish size but the sheer volume of water available without undue bank pressure. The fish you catch are invariable immaculate and much more likely never to have been caught before.

The wind died away, the weather was fine and I was catching good fish with nothing and no-one to spoil my splendid isolation.

Then came the run with a difference! Instead of setting off towards the sluice like its carpy brethren, this one dived for the centre of the canal - and stayed there, doggo! Try as I may, I could not move that fish an inch.

I was beginning to think it had left the hook in a snag, a waterlogged tree, perhaps, or a steam-roller, maybe; for I felt nothing but a solid, immovable resistance. Then, just as I was considering whether to leave the rod in the rests with the anti-reverse off, just to see what happened, or pull for a break, it began to move!

The 2½lb TC rod was already bent double with the reel clutch screwed well down from trying to shift it, but whatever it was took little heed of that and trundled off down towards the sluice gates. Slowly, inexorable it swam down the dead-centre of the waterway, the clutch slowly clicking as it took line, my arms already starting to ache. It crossed my mind it could be a log, now dislodged and being slowly swept downstream. I moved as close to the fence as I could go, grimly hanging on. I looked back the few yards to the landing net. There was no way I could hold the fish with one hand, have the net in the other and climb the fence. It was a big net and I knew, even in the unlikely event of scaling the fence, it would snag on the barbed wire. No, the battle was going to be fought from where I was!

By this time, I was running out of line, the fish, if fish it was, now some one hundred yards downstream and still going! It was now or never. I screwed the clutch down hard hurriedly and was to take a chance in turning this leviathan. Mercifully, the fish began to respond. I held it, in effect, it was by now subject to terrific sidestrain and I was able to start the long retrieve, laboriously pumping it back.

Quite suddenly, I found myself keeping tight contact without pumping. Now I knew it was a fish and I felt elation at the positive knowledge, the fish now swimming upstream towards me! "This was more like it. I was starting to take control", I imagined. When it gets up here, I'll show it who's gaffer! I even got the net ready.

I should have known better. It was to be a long time yet before I'd need the net.

You couldn't say it was a spectacular fight by normal standards. I mean there was no speed about it. All it did was swim up to me - and despite trying to stop it in its tracks - kept going as though I wasn't there! In fact, without any deviation from its chosen path, I had to ease the clutch off until it took line again. I had no choice but to let it go, the clutch resuming its now familiar clicking. I was sweating now and my arms ached intolerable as it ploughed on upstream. I wondered just what the hell I had hooked into - a submarine!

Joking aside, this was really something to get excited about. Whatever monster there was down there, it had no intention of responding to anything I had to offer, as yet. It simply swam on, seemingly unperturbed, relentless, determined. An unease came over me, hard to define, but real. I began to doubt if I would ever master that fish.

A gremlin on my shoulder whispered in my ear, "These canal carp have softer mouths than those at home. Be careful or the hook will pull out!" I pushed the negative thoughts out of my mind, and as the fish was as far upstream as it had been down, I turned it again.

Eventually, it was over the spot where if had originally 'played dead' on the bottom - and despite the bomb, line drag and clutch - again it headed for the sluice. It was back where the whole process had started.

The fish and I did two more complete action replays of the first cycle before I thought I detected a weakening of the fish. On its fourth run downstream I decided that the next time it tried to pass by me I'd give it some stick! I'd start to get to grips with it. That slight uneasy feeling returned and the fear of the hook pulling became an anxiety I could not escape. A dark cloud was gathering. Just as sometimes you know all will be well, so sometimes you sense and dread the inevitable. On that fourth run up to me I at last fought down my doubt and fear and prepared for battle!

I had a chance here, I told myself, of a huge fish, a monster; the kind you dream about, spend years hoping for, the kind that turns every other fish into a minnow: one that makes the whole fishing saga worthwhile. A photograph to enlarge, frame and keep as a symbol of success, of happy days and a love of angling. A great story to tell when age bars you from fishing any more. The fish of a lifetime!

I was still hard in touch as at came level, that fish and I in a world in which only she and I existed. It was more now to me than a fishing adversary, we were at war!

So, foolishly, as planned, I took the initiative and met the fish with as much resistance as I could to hold it in the area. It was, you must understand, even then, about fifteen or twenty feet out. I was immediately rewarded by the most powerful wrench of the rod I have ever experienced. I could not believe a freshwater fish could be so powerful. I mean, POWERFUL! There was a mighty shuddering wrench at the rod as the water roiled and boiled, black ooze throwing up weed, sticks and debris. I wanted to see that fish in the clouds of inky silt, yearned to see it, to catch a glimpse of tail or fin, but even as the last shuddering yanking at the rod took place the cold hand of defeat gripped my angling soul. I knew than I would lose it, had no chance of mastering it.

Suddenly, the line went slack, sprang back towards me, and even though I half expected it, the surprise and shock stunned me into head-shaking disbelief at such a fish!

Without even taking the line out of the water I put the rod on its rests and slumped down in the bedchair, utterly disappointed, gutted. My hands shook as I poured out a cup of flask tea and lit a cigarette. The water was placid again, so ordinary was the scene. I had made contact with the abnormal and had lost. I needed someone to scream at!

Eventually, I got around to blaming myself; what else could I have done? I didn't know. Self-condemnatory thoughts ran riot in my brain, but one sickening though prevailed - and it's still there to this day. I would never know.

I could not even begin to assess its size nor what it was. Not once had I been able to lift it in the water. I'd had no glimpse of it to give me a clue.

Above all, that fish, not for a second did anything at all it did not want to do. When it decided enough was enough, its energy exploded into uncontrollable power, its ponderous bulk unleashing fury at being tethered, regaining its freedom.

The cup empty, I sighed deeply. I stopped gazing hopelessly into space and made an attempt to start again.

I reeled the tackle in, the bomb swinging to my free hand, and I checked the end rig for wear and tear. The hook was broken! Broken - not pulled out nor even opened out, but snapped off on the bend! Kaput!

I couldn't believe it of a make of hook I had always had faith in, and a forged number two at that! Maybe if I'd used a four or a six it might have bitten deeper for I could only assume the two had its point lodged on a gristly or bony part of the fish, the hook having never penetrated at all and the subsequent force applied twixt point and eye snapped it in half!

I cursed the pillock who had forged that hook and failed to set the temper properly. After all, a forged number two is a formidable hook to savage like that. Then I turned my unreasonable wrath on the packer, the seller, responsible for off-loading it on an unsuspecting angler, while all the time I knew who the real culprit was. I had known those hooks were mass produced, had known the probability of there being at least one faulty in a box of a hundred. I should have tested it myself!

Later I tested them all that were left and could find none wanting. What was it then that made me pick out one dodgy hook from so many? Was it fate, pure chance, Sod's Law or what? I didn't know then and I still don't know now.

Such a small item of tackle, a hook. All the time and money, all the skill and knowledge, all made irrelevant by one hook.

Ah well! That's fishing for you! You know, fishing's such a personal sport whether you fish alone or in a crowd. Just suppose I'd banked that fish, would the memory of the day be so vivid? Would it all have been so indelibly imprinted in the heart of me, I wonder?

I do have a tale to tell in my dotage. There's no photograph, mind, to hang on the wall. But I do have a story of a fish of a lifetime, the one that got away....!

Every angler should have one of those!

Shadows On The Lake

There are still areas of Lincolnshire where technology has yet to rip away the character of the landscape; where dragonfly dances at the tip of reed and rush, silently tracing the edge of still waters. Flight paths of a different kind once knew the drone of Lancasters, set to drop their sticks of death on a foreign land, now holding the reverberations of monster, triangular Vulcans who cast their shadows on the lake - so near, so close - yet in a million miles apart from this 'reality', this placid peaceful lake.

F for Freddie and V for Victor flew and fly that I might savour sight and sound of moorhen, vole and fish! That I might remember.

The April evening had about it a breathlessness only the falling away of a coastal breeze can bring, while the cuckoo from afar showed strain from constant canting. The croon of a soon-to-roost wood-pigeon added to the soft chatter of countless smaller birds. The squabble of water birds and the lone pheasant call were the same as ever - but where have all the jackdaws gone?

Distant dogs barked from time to time while a young blood, hellbent on two wheels, could be heard doing his Barry Sheene through the gearbox, so very far away. Where waited his Olivia Newton John?

The mirror finish on the water reflected a clear inversion of the surrounding poplar, elm, willow and hawthorn, while behind me the sun weakened as it fell into another sea across the land, beyond the crazy cacophony that is Blackpool. The fools! They could be here with me! I thanked God they were not.

Recheck everything - for the magic hour is nigh. Anti-reverses on, bail arms shut. I trace the lines from bail-arm rollers down to indicators, up through butt rings and antennae and beyond to dip in a gentle slope to dimple the surface tension of the water, sealing below the mysterious underwater world, a world as remote from mine as the disciplined world of flight technology overhead.

Imperceptible, the light begins to dim and the first carp of the evening shakes out of the water some fifty yards away. Excitement rises. Anticipation is heightened and intensified by the utter stillness - the hush of evening. There is a sense of timelessness, a recognition of the complexity of nature and the temporary span of man's existence; almost, but not quite, an understanding of life itself.

The baits were near the end of a bar, the bar, where it began, fringed with reeds. Where it terminated out in the middle a triangle of tree-stumps rose out of shallow water, their gnarled and twisted roots snaking into the old clay workings. Where now those hands that dug the pit so long ago? Occasionally a fish knifes the water around the roots, the carp safe in their sanctuary.

I check the lines yet again and know, with the baits so close to those snags, I'd have to be quick in taking up any ensuing battle, or they'd be under the tree-roots before I'd got the rod up! I mentally rehearse where I can strike safely without fouling the bushes and trees behind me and look where I can land a fish some ten yards to my right.

Nothing happens and time ticks on. Concentration wanes a little. As the dusk deepens, everything is so still, even an insect alighting on the line would cause a ripple on the elastic surface. My thoughts wander....Maggie Thatcher's world intrudes....work conditions....family and friends come to mind....That's a tail out there! I wonder if carp are aware of me....My mind goes back, when as a boy in short pants I fished with a home-maid quill float and I 'see' it again rise up and topple flat before sliding away after a slab of bream in true Mr Crabtree style. That was a time when Glen Miller was in full swing and Land Army girls made hay!

Splioo..oosh! My reverie is broken by a great golden-flanked body rising out of the water, up on its tail, not three yards out. It crashes back in a belly flop that actually showered me with drops of spray. She rises up yet again and repeats the performance.

"Good Grief, did you see that?" I asked nobody.

Waves from the disturbance lap against the banksticks and have barely subsided when the right-hand buzzer howls and the indicator shoots up the stick. My calm appraisal of the scene is forgotten in that blind, blank, heart-stopping moment when the rod is swept up and back. The line rips out of the water and I feel the jerk of the fish at my arms as I forget my worked-out-plan-of-action, forget vivid and detailed descriptions of masterclass writings; forget how people claim to set the hook, anticipate every move of the fish, give and take line at the right moments, raise and lower the rod to exact every ounce of advantage and power from the blank.

Instead, I step back and almost fall over the bedchair in my wellies. Then I stumble along the bank to heave the threshing fish away from those roots. And I'm not happy until I'm sure it can't get back.

Forgotten is the poetry of motion of curved rod against the sky in that explosion of activity. I hang on and feel the surge of power as it bores away, mercifully into open water. It would be nice to say I sank the rod tip and applied sidestrain and turned the fish where I wanted it to go, but it went of its own accord.

The adrenalin is really pumping now and I do actually begin to enjoy the sheer pleasure of playing the fish 'to the manner born'. It takes line from the clutch and sets off again towards the roots but I've gained too much for it ever to get back there again. I gently screw down on the clutch and hold the fish some thirty yards out.

Now, I _know_ that I shall win. I _know_ this fish will not shake the hook, nor part the line, just as I _know_ I shall soon cradle it in my arms. How do I know these things? Well, sometimes, you just _do_! It bores deep as it nears the net, giving one last surge in an attempt to get free. For the first time I wonder how big is it? It boils to the surface and looks good as it slips into the net and is hauled clear of the water.

The weigh-sling is duly wetted and the scale reads sixteen-ten. My first carp - and a good double, a nice mirror, as it says in the books. A fish to be remembered. More moments to be savoured as it slides from my hands into the water. With one powerful thrust of its tail, it is gone!

My heart had slowed its pumping a little, but, stupidly, my hands are shaking a bit. How daft can you get? Over a fish! And funny where so many people have appeared from to look, share the moment....perhaps envy a little.

Later, when dusk has given way to darkness, when sun has given way to moon and stars, new sounds enrich the lake. Alone again, I savoured every second of the first carp. I relived an action replay, smiling at my initial antics and my panic but snug and smug in my bedchair I enjoyed the satisfaction it had brought me.

I watched the lone aircraft as it droned across the night sky, its navigation lights winking to the stars as it traced its invisible patrol route. I marvelled at the ancient flight-paths of the planets. Was Star Wars yet to come? I wondered if the pilot had had a memorable day - and did he like to fish? And for sure, when he and I were gone, would it not be that men would fly those selfsame flight paths in different shapes - but would the dragonfly and fish be there, that was the question?

There were shadows on the lake.

The Stream Of Life

The journey takes just over an hour. At that time of the morning the roads are almost devoid of traffic; traffic lights controlling ghost vehicles, the shiny, wet street waiting for daylight to transform them from dimly lit caverns of emptiness to an intensity of ant-like activity as the sun sweeps away the fluorescent beams and dark recesses.

In the suburbs, the unmistakable outline of an angler with his tackle is seen against the backdrop of a whitewashed wall. There, hunched against the morning, he awaits transport to speed him to another spot, there to fish the day away. I hope his mates turn up!

I travel a familiar route out of the built-up area, accelerating eagerly down the slip road onto the broad, three-lane by-pass, my mind divided between almost automatic car control and the anticipation of things yet to come.

The husky female voice of the 'trucker's friend' invites from the radio, while the wipers, set slow, clear the mist from the windscreen. The songs she plays, just for you, are alien to this environment, yet familiar. They tell tales of other highways in other places in cross-Atlantic drawls as predictable guitars play predictable riffs between predictable lyrics.

My mind registers ten thousand illusory impingements on its mirror but is actually tuned to its own predictable thoughts. 'The swim - will it be free? Have I baited up for some other sod to reap the benefit? Even if it is free, will it be the place to fish? Had I remembered my flask? I'll have a good look round first - look for signs.'

The white V on a massive blue board indicates departure from the three-lane dronezone into the uneven streets of a Northern town, still ambered by the Electricity

Board, holding a steady auric glow against the sky. A corner turned and I'm in another world. Well, almost another world. Town and country are rolled into one here. At the bottom of the slope on the near side lies a man-made water, a reservoir to serve the Industrial Revolution. It once fed a lone works amid a severely green landscape, but is now nearly swallowed up by brick and mortar, the population explosion having eaten at the heart of rural England.

Strangely, though surrounded by roads and buildings, once at the waterside, much of the concrete jungle is hidden from view. Oddly, there is a profusion of trees and bushes; and while something less than half of the water is contained in concrete walling, the rest of it appears to be natural banking. However, I say appears, because a bankstick pierces the wafer-thin turf to grate on rock, shingle, brick and shale.

There is plenty of weed and large area of reed, and apart from the right-angled corner it is irregular in shape, so for all the world it looks as though a lake has been dropped into a concrete recess in the earth. By town standards, it is a pleasant place to be! From the car you can immediately see if swims are occupied. If there are no cars at the kerb, you are in!

I am alone as I open the car boot and begin the ritual. Struggling into a one-piece suit, half-in and half-out of a pair of wellies, dancing precariously on one foot, a police patrol-car draws up alongside, complete with glossy insignia. The nearside window is wound down and I can read the minds of the two officers inside, two peas in a pod. "'Ello, 'ello, 'ello, they think to themselves, what's going on here?" I don't blame them, I suppose. After all, a car parked up with the boot open at four in the morning is a mite suspicious. They now see I am a fisherman and the face of the nearest officer changes perceptibly, smiles. There is still, however, a hint of doubt behind the smile. "Been here all night, mate?"
Had I committed a traffic violation or been dressed in a decent suit, he was likely to address me as sir! But he was only doing his job, making sure.

"No, just arrived," I said, managing to get my foot into the other welly without falling over.

"You fishing then?"

"Yes," I reply to the obvious.

"You're and early bird, I'll give you that!"

"You have to be," I said, not wishing to explain the complexity of reasons to a non-angler.

That bemused and baffled look of the philistine when trying to fathom the warped priorities of an angler showed clearly in his face.

"Well," he said politely, "Good luck!"

The window winds back up and the two heads shake in bewilderment, the glass and the engine cutting off the beginnings of laughter.

"Good luck! I'll need it!" I mutter to myself, getting the rest of the gear out and locking the boot.

By the time I get to my swim, get set up, two rods out, and a cup of tea to add a final touch of pleasure, dawn has crept up on me. It's a fine, still morning, the placid lake only disturbed by waterbirds, roach rings and angler's lines, for others had now arrived.

The roads, mainly out of sight had begun to issue a growing volume of traffic noise and the necklace of amber lights above the by-pass are almost faded into the sky. A factory chimney rises triumphant above the skyline like some great phallic symbol of man's success over his environment; and a large cloud of white, cumulus smoke sits on top of this brick pinnacle, still and unchanging, the whole resembling an enormous candyfloss.

The string of cars at the kerbside has lengthened, some sleek and new, some old and battered. A rusty van announces the arrival of two good friends, one of them, as I write, now, sadly, deceased.

The intrepid anglers commence their own ritual, seeking roach, pike or carp, each according to his thing.

"'Ad any runs?" the carp boys ask as they stop to survey the water, glancing down at you gear, hoping, perhaps, to gain a bait clue.

"'Ad owt?" the box-laden roach lads enquire, as though my activity was likely to bear any correlation to theirs!

They all tramp like refugees from an Everest expedition. My discouraging grunts fail to wipe the hope from their eyes, nor alter their eager, clomping gait.

From the carp's point of view, it must have looked like a camel train etched against the skyline and noise level copied Clapham Junction in the rush hour. Has no-one read Walker's Stillwater Angling except yours truly?

Later, the news starts to travel round the banks: "Jim 'ad a nineteen plus common last Tuesday...Harry's 'ad three doubles this week, the jammy devil!...Did you read that bit about Yatesy?...The twenty-two's been out again...Dunno, some bloke from Brum, they reckon"...and so on.

The sound of thwacking catapults off the concrete wall announces the arrival of two friends, two of the most successful on the water. Quickly and efficiently, they go about their business. I watch the baits plop into a tight area with rhythmic regularity. It's time now to sit and wait, all day, if necessary - but who knows, the action may come to anyone at any time - or no-one!

The piping of adjusted Optonics pierces the general noise level like a flute superimposes on a wave of orchestral sound.

A young lad wanders up, a boy really, already impatient, perhaps, at the lack of action. "'Ad any runs?" he asks abruptly with seeming innocent candour. Even though I might wish to be alone with my thoughts, I don't want to discourage the young. I owe too much to elder who taught me the fishing game, when I was his age.
"No, not yet," I answer pleasantly.
"What bait are you on, mister?"
My reply was meant to suggest, even if I told him, he could not possibly understand what I was talking about. He had asked the question only friends and confidants had a right to ask. The young ask it - or the fool.
"Oh, it's one I make up myself." I was not now quite sure of his 'innocence'. Had a crafty devil of a brother sent him, I wondered? He gave up and went.

A carp rolled out in the middle. Carpmen could be seen standing and pointedly looking at the spot, lest it might be thought of them that they missed the incident. No-one had a bait in that area.

It looked like being one of those mornings when nothing happens but the occasional sighting of a carp, the occasional wandering from swim to swim 'for a natter', the occasional clank and clang from the nearby works, the occasional drink of flask-tea, and the occasional relief of bladder pressure.

A slight breeze drifts the candyfloss smoke from the towering chimney and ruffles the water in irregular patches. I drop into a state of reverie, of relaxed awareness every angler knows so well.

I'm back to an age when I asked searching questions and looked with envy at the tackle grown men used, far back from the industrially spawned water...

The journey to the venue was different then. Only a few well-off fathers had cars, mind. It was an era of shank's pony for me! We set out in those hazy, lazy days of summer, holidaying from school in wartime Britain, not knowing much of the worked, but able to tell the difference between Spitfire, Messerschmitt, Hurricane and Focke-Wolfe; still too young to employ our boyish energy on potato-picking safaris into the flatlands of the Fen, yet old enough to walk the three miles to the nearest village, rod in hand, its centre-pin reel permanently lashed to the butt with sugar-string whippings.

Full of hope, we would leave the little market town behind on its hill, our pockets bulging with a tobacco-tin full of tackle and other schoolboy necessities of life. The maggots we carried had been salvaged from a rotting fish or rabbit carcass buried in the garden; a garden rich in natural food. It was Dig for Victory time!

Sometimes an army lorry would pass us by on the dusty road, hot with bubbling tarmac. Now and then a whole convoy roared past, the soldiers carrying with them full packs and issue, their rifles between their knees or propped up against the tailboard with its strange regimental signs. We could not know how much we were envied by those troops - nor where they were going...

Our victory was to be over dace and gudgeon from

a tiny, winding beck, a stream, a ribbon of water chuckling its way through fields of golden corn, lush, green meadows of grazing sheep and cattle, its varied banks rich in wildlife and decorated with hawthorn, willow, bramble and gorse. On occasions, rarely more than one in a schoolboy lifetime, someone hooked a trout, an escape from the slowly eddying millpool in the village that beckoned us on. The weathered notice there said: PRIVATE - NO FISHING. But we would gaze longingly at the pool, none daring to fish there, not in the daytime - and then not until we were somewhat older. But that's another story.

No, our allotted place started from the weir on the other side of the bridge, from which point we trotted our lines for two miles downstream to link with another roadbridge, at which point we headed for home. Thus, in effect, our trek was triangular with home as the apex and the winding river the base.

Every trip we would pray to catch one of those lovely trout - they were all of a pound in weight - but like most things in those days, they were not easy to come by. We thought of them as being the ultimate experience in fishing, as indeed, for us, they were! There was no telly, no angling books or papers available to us and no money to call our own. Our angling world was that little stream, the two-mile stretch, as we and it meandered through the edge of the Wolds. Where it came from, or where it went, we knew not. Such thoughts did not arise when to experience and savour the present was sufficient for the day.

There were no secrets then: all things were shared - and we had been taught our craft well by men who knew the land and waters, for they, too, had trodden those selfsame paths before us.

Thus, at a tender age, we were 'experts' in our angling world. We layed-on, stret-pegged, long-trotted and swam the stream without knowing the technical jargon, and we learnt every inch of that running water. It was never more than three feet deep, and only then when it doubled back on itself in a wide sweep, to find the softest route, biting deep into the banks of sandy soil.

In most places, you had less then six inches depth to deal with, and from shallows, gravel beds, rapids and eddying backwaters we took dace, gudgeon and Miller's thumbs, eels now and then, and those elusive trout.

We could trot the water with tatty tackle in all conditions and glean from it all it had to yield, rarely snagging or losing precious hooks in streamer weed. We knew instantly whether the ultra rapid bites came from delicately marked gudgeon or the mercurial dace, and we could stalk the saturday-matinee red Indians into the ground!

But there were times when even the magic of a dancing float gave way to her pursuits as we Huckleberry Finned our way downstream to the next bridge.

At the very outset, we knew we would stop halfway at the old, broken-down barn-shed, its ancient wood splintering from years of exposure to sun, wind, rain and ice. There, we would seek and find the loosely matted blackie nests or the mud-lined saucer holding the gaping chicks of the speckled thrush, the odd bit of black squiggled blue eggshell remaining. House martins and swallows dived in and out, arguing who was to be cowboy and who Indian. Sometimes we just rested awhile in the straw, wishing we had some pop!

We whooped after fleeing rabbits, put to flight from beneath corn stalks. Nettling our bare knees when we fell with dockleaf and our own spit, we tried to be as stoical as Geronimo, but usually failed!

Nearby was the sandy river bank where sand martins lived, deep in their holes, and deeper still the flashing kingfisher; and we searched for the cosy, horsehair nests of linnet and yellowhammer among the gorse bushes, trying not to heed the prickles. Before moving on we would pluck the burrs from our stockings, perhaps catching sight of a heron silently stood immobile, waiting for its dinner, or flapping awkwardly as it winged away.

Farther downstream little kids scooped minnows with their pathetic sixpenny nets, transferring them to jam-jars with string for a handle. We scoffed at their efforts. Already, we were specimen hunters and did not know it!

The rising larks we took for granted as they soared on high above crow, pheasant and whirling lapwing, but we never took for granted that cows were not bulls, if you know what I mean!

We had many an Oxford and Cambridge boat-race and 'bombed' a few German pocket battleships with clods of good English soil; and it was pretty certain one or more of us would get wet before the day was out. Chasing a butterfly or two, seeing dancing goldfinches on thistle heads and maybe catching sight of an old dog fox on his rounds was all part and parcel of goin' fishin' - instead of just a'wishin'!

Yet the clammy hand of commercialism intruded into even that paradise. Italian prisoners-of-war worked the nearby farms, and we quickly learned these swarthy foreigners, in their baggy, yellow-patched suits, had peculiar culinary tastes.

We traded with them. The going rate, five gudgeon equalled one Woodbine! Our return to the water unharmed principle was conveniently forgotten. Of course, you didn't tell your Dad of these transactions.

So, we John Wayned our way home, climbing wearily up the hill back to town, our bellies telling us we were late. We puffed and panted along uncut verges, a veritable nature-trail in their own right, buzzing with life. Bumble bees sucked the clover heads dry and grasshoppers abounded in the long summer grasses. It was a bit too much cissy to give the buttercup, daisy and forget-me-not more than a passing glance. Eventually, we near the old Norman church, though its tower had been in sight much of the way. We had listened to the clock chimes to see if we were to get a verbal drubbing - or worse!

I look at my watch. The day half gone and nobody catching from the stillwater. Suddenly it looks exactly what it is, being pleasant recognised as being only relatively so. Everything now seems greyer, grimy. The litter-strewn banks, I know, are rat infested at night. The background traffic din seems louder now and there are anglers every few yards right round the water - far too many! I sigh for lost youth and better days. My keenness gone, it's time for a natter. I reel the lines in and set off to seek out friends.

On the way, behind a bush, I see the boy, his 'innocence' now destroyed. He's as near ultra-cult as makes no difference, a pair of matched twelve foot carbons, that make now in vogue, endorsed by a 'name' angler as a result of a catch thousands of miles from this insipid water. Converted Optonics, bedchair, bivy - the lot! He looks up.

"What bait are you on?" I ask with wry good humour. He misses the fact I'm having a good-natured dig at him, so I smile to show no ill-will.

"Bog off!" he snarls, his face etched with a scowl that has no place on a boy; not a boy fishing, that's for sure. The grimace on his face would have done many a television 'hero' proud.

There is a gulf between us for which neither is to blame. I feel the anger within me. Not at him so much, but at those in society who have produced a schoolboy cynic. Neither of us is to blame for that. The anger subsides. After all, how can he know or understand? Anymore than we could know the thoughts of those soldiers in the army trucks so long ago!

Further Reading

Arbery, Len. *Catching Big Tench*. (David and Charles).

Arbery, Len, and Clifford, Kevin. *The Redmire Pool*. (Beekay).

Haines, Alan. *The Complete Book of Float Fishing*. (David and Charles).

Little, Andy. *Big Carp Fishing*. (Hamlyn).

Maddocks, Kevin. *Carp Fever*. (Beekay).

Miles, Tony. *The Complete Specimen Hunter*. (Crowood Press).

Phillips, Roger, and Rix, Martyn. *Freshwater Fish of Britain, Irelaned and Europe*. (Pan Press).

Walker, Falcus, Buller and Taylor. *Successful Angling*. (Stanley Paul).

Useful Addresses

Carp Anglers Association
Membership Secretary
Castle Cary Press
High Street
Castle Cary
Somerset
BA7 7AN

The Carp Society
33 Covert Road
Hainault
Ilford
Essex

Index

additives, 42, 43, 51-52.
Arbery, Len, 75, 76, 97, 99, 105.

baitdroppers, 46.
Berners, Dame Juliana, 8.
boats and rafts, 46.
bottom fishing, 79.
buying a reel, 31, 32.

catapults, 45, 131.
choosing a rod, 29, 37.
choosing line, 37.
Clifford, Kevin, 97.

ducker floats, 65-66

feeding aids, 44.
Fish:
      barbel, 21, 49-51, 69, 103, 104.
      bream, 50, 68, 89-93, 110-112, 125.
      carp, 17, 20, 21, 23, 50, 52-54, 59, 60, 66, 76, 80, 83, 84,
          95-102, 105, 112, 118, 119, 121, 125-127, 130-132.
      chub, 49, 50, 69, 76, 87, 102, 104.
      crayfish, 20.
      perch, 20, 76, 89, 91, 93-95, 102, 103, 108-112, 115, 116.
      pike, 17, 22, 40, 47, 71, 72, 79, 94, 95, 101, 102, 113, 114,
          130.
      roach, 53, 69, 76, 88-91, 95, 110, 111, 113, 114, 130.
      stickleback, 20.
      tench, 23, 50, 54, 66, 75, 76, 80, 90, 104-107, 111.
fish identification, 61.
fish stealing, 17.

Haines, Allan, 63.
Hindley, Jim, 92, 93.

keepnets, 50.
Knots:
     Billy Lane, 40.
     grinner, 38, 40, 82.
     overhand, 40.
     palomar, 40.
     paternoster, 40, 44, 49, 72, 73, 77-80, 82, 92, 94, 102.
     spade whipping, 39.

legering, 23, 33, 34, 38, 40, 49, 59, 73, 81, 85, 86, 92, 95, 101.
leger rods, 29, 86.
link leger, 81, 82.
Little, Andy, 100.

Maddocks, Kevin, 52, 84, 99.
mixing bait, 43.

oyster, 20.

polution 17.
prebaiting, 50, 51.

rod action, 27, 103.

shotting, 63, 64, 69, 71, 100.
stopstick, 73, 74.
swimfeeders, 40, 45.

throwing sticks, 45, 46, 122.

waggler style, 44, 63-65, 67, 68, 70, 71, 76, 106, 107.
Walker, Richard, 9, 13, 75, 98, 99, 112, 131.
Whipp, Nicholas, 87.

zoomer fishing, 70.

Angler's Record

Date	Time	Location	Fish	Weight

Angler's Record

Date	Time	Location	Fish	Weight

Angler's Record

Date	Time	Location	Fish	Weight